CORPORATE UNIVERSITIES

Organizations constantly need to adapt themselves to stay aligned with an ever-changing and increasingly complex environment. *Corporate Universities* puts "smart learning" at the forefront, with strategies to secure alignment between organization and environment, which need both speed of learning and learning in the right direction. Across the globe, corporate universities have emerged as vehicles of such strategy-driven learning.

Corporate Universities bridges the gap between the disciplines of strategic management and corporate learning, combining general strategy with the concept of corporate universities, which, to date, has predominantly been an HR topic. Readers will find new concepts, as well as generic corporate university strategies to link corporate strategy to organizational learning. In-depth cases show how corporate universities are used to renew, transform, and optimize strategy and include important lessons learned by corporate university executives, from both small and global companies, as well as governmental organizations across different industries.

Written for academics in strategy, HRD, and organizational behavior disciplines, as well as practicing managers alike, *Corporate Universities* is the first book that offers a consistent set of concepts, frameworks, and cases to integrate general strategy with organizational learning.

Martyn F. Rademakers is Managing Director of the Center for Strategy & Leadership and has been a Research Associate at the Rotterdam School of Management, Erasmus University, Rotterdam.

CORPORATE UNIVERSITIES

Drivers of the learning organization

Martyn F. Rademakers

LONDON AND NEW YORK

First published 2014
by Routledge
2 Park Square, Milton Park, Abingdon, Oxon OX14 4RN

and by Routledge
711 Third Avenue, New York, NY 10017

Routledge is an imprint of the Taylor & Francis Group, an informa business

© 2014 Martyn F. Rademakers

The right of Martyn F. Rademakers to be identified as author of this work has been asserted by him in accordance with sections 77 and 78 of the Copyright, Designs and Patents Act 1988.

All rights reserved. No part of this book may be reprinted or reproduced or utilized in any form or by any electronic, mechanical, or other means, now known or hereafter invented, including photocopying and recording, or in any information storage or retrieval system, without permission in writing from the publishers.

Trademark notice: Product or corporate names may be trademarks or registered trademarks, and are used only for identification and explanation without intent to infringe.

British Library Cataloguing in Publication Data
A catalogue record for this book is available from the British Library

Library of Congress Cataloging in Publication Data
Rademakers, Martyn.
  Corporate universities : drivers of the learning organization/Martyn F. Rademakers.
    page cm
  1. Employer-supported education. 2. Employees—Training of.
  3. Organizational learning. 4. Knowledge management. I. Title.
  HF5549.5.T7R235 2014
  658.3'124—dc23   2013030757

ISBN: 978-0-415-66054-9 (hbk)
ISBN: 978-0-415-73770-8 (pbk)
ISBN: 978-0-203-07398-8 (ebk)

Typeset in Bembo
by RefineCatch Limited, Bungay, Suffolk

For Kris, Eva, and Bas, from whom I learn so much, every day

CONTENTS

List of illustrations	*viii*
About the author and the co-authors	*x*
Acknowledgments	*xii*
1. Introduction: Corporate Universities	1
2. Strategy Development for Continuous Learning	10
3. Corporate University Strategy	25
4. Corporate University Value Creation and Learning Formats	38
5. Mars University: Raising the Bar	53
6. Deloitte University: Developing as One	68
7. Shell Project Academy: Developing a Learning Community	77
8. Canon Academy: Accelerating Transformation	92
9. Corporate University Strategy Renewal at ING	103
10. Bringing Speed to Knowledge: A Dean's Journey	113
11. Corporate University Definitions, Literature, and Lessons Learned	127
Index	*151*

ILLUSTRATIONS

Figures

1.1	Overview of the eleven chapters and their focus	2
2.1	Aligning the market system and the business system	12
2.2	Alignment between business system and organizational system	14
2.3	Alignment between organization system and personal system	17
2.4	Forms of continuous learning	20
2.5	Levels of strategy specificity	22
3.1	Exploitation versus exploration	27
3.2	School, College, and Academy strategies and the primal forms of organizational strategy	31
3.3	Playing the average game	33
3.4	(Re)focused corporate university strategies	33
3.5	Disentangling the corporate university	34
4.1	Corporate university Value Creation Menu	39
4.2	Corporate university Learning Formats Model	43
5.1	The Five Mars Principles	55
5.2	Work streams for Mars University development	60
5.3	Overview of six Mars tenets of success and actions	62
6.1	The Deloitte Learning Platform	72
7.1	Top eight oil and gas companies in the world, with their relative shares in the aggregate annual revenue 2011	78
7.2	Upstream, midstream, and downstream activities in the oil and gas industry	79
7.3	Image of the SPA Pentagon	83
7.4	The Shell Project Academy governance structure	86
8.1	Canon regions	94

Illustrations **ix**

8.2	Kyosei in Japanese characters	95
8.3	From strategy to implementation – adopting Key Account Management (KAM)	98
9.1	The Leadership Pipeline	105
9.2	ING Business School evolution	110
10.1	Philips Lighting levels of certification	119
10.2	Getting and keeping knowledge up to speed	122
10.3	Overview of a dean's journey, 1998–2014	125
11.1	Shifting corporate university strategies at Mars University	134
11.2	Generic strategies of ING Business School and ING Bank Academy	136
11.3	Shell Project Academy generic strategies over time	137
11.4	Generic strategy of Canon Academy	139
11.5	Generic strategy of Deloitte University	140
11.6	SCA strategies of Philips Lighting University	141
11.7	Comparing and contrasting strategy specificity	143
11.8	Shaping factors for a strategic corporate university profile	144
11.9	Variation in performance tracking styles of the corporate universities	144

Exhibits

4.1	Company profiles of Heineken, Ahold, and TNT	45
5.1	Emerging corporate education in China	56
5.2	Overview of Mars University Leadership Development programs	63
6.1	Brain-based learning at Deloitte	72
7.1	The Shell Project delivery process benchmark	81
7.2	The Desired World in Project Land	81
7.3	SPA performance indicators	87
9.1	The pull approach	106
10.1	Creating "pull" and output control through certification	121

Tables

3.1	School, College, and Academy business system characteristics	30
6.1	Number of people employed at Deloitte, breakdown per region	69
11.1	Corporate university definitions	128

ABOUT THE AUTHOR AND THE CO-AUTHORS

Martyn F. Rademakers PhD is Managing Director of the Center for Strategy & Leadership, an internationally operating executive education and consulting company based in the Netherlands. Martyn has been a Research Associate at the Rotterdam School of Management Erasmus University, Rotterdam, and a Visiting Professor at various business schools in Europe and Asia. He is a co-founder and board member of the Dutch Foundation for Corporate Universities.

Ron Meyer PhD is Professor of Corporate Strategy at TiasNimbas Business School, Tilburg University, and Managing Director of the Center for Strategy & Leadership. His research is focused on the connection between strategy development and leadership, with a strong emphasis on the role of top management in driving corporate learning.

Ron authored Chapter 2 about strategy and co-authored Chapter 4 about corporate university value creation and learning formats.

Han van der Pool is a corporate university veteran with more than thirty years of experience gained during his work at international organizations in the public, logistic, manufacturing, retail, academic, and consultancy sectors in the USA, Europe, Asia Pacific, and Africa.

Han co-authored Chapter 4 about corporate university value creation and learning formats.

Paul Hunter DBA is Founder and Chief Executive of the Strategic Management Institute based in Melbourne, Australia. He is a frequent speaker, educator, and provider of executive education courses on strategy. He is currently authoring a book on strategy practice, titled *The 7 Inconvenient Truths of Strategy*.

Paul co-authored Chapter 5 about Mars University.

About the author and the co-authors

Nick van Dam PhD is Chief Learning Officer, Global Talent for Deloitte Touche Tohmatsu Limited. He is an internationally recognized consultant, author, speaker, and thought leader on organizational learning & leadership development.

Nick co-authored Chapter 6 about Deloitte University.

Bill Pelster is Principal in the Deloitte Consulting LLP Human Capital Practice leading integrated talent strategies. He is the former CLO of Deloitte.

Bill co-authored Chapter 6 about Deloitte University.

Hans Wierda is the Functional Director of Major Projects in Centrica Energy, Windsor, UK, and responsible for Project Management Assurance and Competence Development. He led the development, implementation, and optimization of the Shell Project Academy between 2006 and 2009.

Hans co-authored Chapter 7 about Shell Project Academy.

Ruud Polet is a veteran in corporate communications leadership development, change, and learning, and former Global Director of ING Business School. Currently, he is responsible for a global Communications & Change program at Royal Philips Electronics to support the creation of a global Corporate University.

Ruud co-authored Chapter 9 about ING Business School/ING Bank Academy.

Carin Termeer is a leadership development professional and executive coach and is known for her deep corporate experience and warm authenticity. Until 2012, she was the Director of Leadership Development of ING Business School.

Carin co-authored Chapter 9 about ING Business School/ING Bank Academy.

ACKNOWLEDGMENTS

The origins of this book stem from curiosity. Coming across the phenomenon of corporate universities for the first time in 2000, they immediately evoked a desire in me to learn more about them. As a strategist, I wondered how corporate universities could contribute to the competitive *and* cooperative strength of organizations. Research on the crossroads of strategy and learning and workshops and conversations with senior managers, corporate university leaders, advisors, and academics helped to figure out some of the answers to my questions. These answers gave rise to new questions and they also triggered ideas and initiatives that led me to write this book.

The process of writing a book is somewhat paradoxical. It is usually a lonely exercise for the author, although it involves many people who are indispensable for its success. This book could not have been written without the knowledge, commitment, craftsmanship, experience, energy, and enthusiasm shared so generously by so many people.

Many examples used in this book are based on corporate university cases authored with the help of Sebastiaan Tampinongkol (Achmea Academy), Marjelle Elema (IND), Ite Smit (Alliantie Academy), Marga Donehoo (DHV University), Baukje Sijpkens, Marion van Barneveld (Corporate Learning Center), Monica de Graaf (VolkerWessels Academy), Arlette Westerhoff (Waternet Academy), Monique van Gurp (Aquademy), Mieke Posthumus, and Pim Verheijen (Dutch Foundation for Corporate Universities). Without their indispensable contributions and support this book would never have been realized.

Ronald van der Molen (Canon Academy), Stefaan van Hooydonk (Philips Lighting University), and Jim Brody (Mars University) invested significant time and energy in the interviews, discussions, and email conversations with me about their corporate universities. Their willingness to unveil their deep knowledge, ideas, and experience with regard to developing and leading exemplary corporate universities is deeply acknowledged.

Ron Meyer (Center for Strategy & Leadership) contributed an elegant chapter about strategy, and he co-authored the chapter on corporate university value creation and learning formats. The book benefits greatly from the clarity of the treatment of strategy and corporate learning which Ron added to the contents.

I also owe gratitude to Han van der Pool, Paul Hunter, Nick van Dam, Bill Pelster, Hans Wierda, Ruud Polet, and Carin Termeer, who co-authored chapters about the corporate universities they have built, led, or been involved in. Thanks to their contributions, the book covers a rich palette of descriptions of the corporate university strategies, structures, and systems, and also inspiring practices, lessons learned, straightforward details, and the challenges faced. It is safe to say that all have invested substantial time in jointly writing many versions of the chapters, which eventually led to the final text. Thank you for your patience and perseverance, and for the knowledge shared. I have learned so much from you.

Lotte Humme and Giancarlo Stanco (Center for Strategy & Leadership) generated most of the figures in this book. Along with a keen eye for telling details, their energy and creativity have been of immense help in getting the graphics right – at any time, even if it meant burning the midnight oil. Apart from that, they assisted in the desk research that the book required.

Most of the chapters in this book have benefited greatly from scrutiny in detail by Joy Christensen, who has masterfully created smooth and clear text out of manuscripts written in American, Australian, and Dutch varieties of the English language.

I am also grateful for the support provided by Marjolein van Altena, Karin Feteris, Johanna Wolfbauer, the followers of #CUbook by @mflrademakers, and the members of the Corporate University Strategy Group on LinkedIn.

Kris, Eva, and Bas Rademakers, thank you for your vital love and support.

Over the years my curiosity about corporate universities has continued to grow, and I hope that will hold true for the book's readers as well. It is a stimulating thought that there is still so much to learn about corporate universities.

Martyn F. Rademakers
Aerdenhout, Netherlands
January 2014

1
INTRODUCTION: CORPORATE UNIVERSITIES

> Genius without education
> is like silver in the mine.
> −Benjamin Franklin

The number of corporate universities around the world is rising. Thousands of publicly listed corporations and privately held and state-owned companies, as well as family businesses and non-profit and semi-governmental organizations, have established their own corporate universities or they are in the process of developing one.[1] The size of the organization does not matter much. Among the smallest companies with a fully-fledged corporate university is Enclos Corp, an American firm with a workforce of about 450 people,[2] while Russian Railways (RZD), employing about 1.3 million people, is among the largest.[3]

Counter-intuitively, the interest in corporate universities seems to have been on the rise since the dawn of the worldwide economic crisis in 2008. This development can be seen both in emerging and declining economies and both among companies affected by the economic downturn, as well as those taking advantage of it. The development is contrary to the dotcom crisis of 2000–2001 when, generally speaking, the corporate university concept was in its infancy. Yet, rather than being acknowledged as a strategic asset, many corporate universities were seen as a me-too or an experiment inspired by early adopters, such as General Electric.[4] Now, 12 years down the road, companies have clear strategic reasons to establish, develop, or maintain a corporate university. A variety of the strategic reasons can be found in this book.

The next ten chapters offer a range of examples and in-depth cases about companies from different continents, countries, and industries (most of them successful, but some that are facing hardship) and the role of their corporate universities in *renewing, implementing, and optimizing strategy*. Moreover, the book pairs

Overview and summary of the chapters

Each chapter in this book revolves around the strategic role of corporate universities. Figure 1.1 provides a condensed overview of the chapters and their focus. As depicted in the figure, the book is divided into three parts: Part I provides concepts, theory, and instruments for the design of business strategy and strategies for corporate universities. The heart of the book, Part II, which contains six in-depth cases about different corporate universities, reveals the direct connection between strategy and organizational learning. All of the chapters in this part of the book take the strategic needs of the companies as their point of departure. Brief introductions to the companies and industries involved are provided as a context for the description of corporate university strategies, structures, practices, challenges,

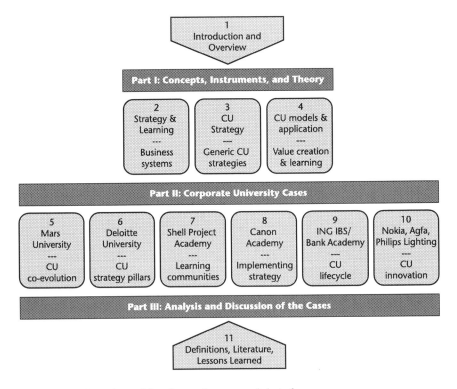

FIGURE 1.1 Overview of the eleven chapters and their focus

and lessons learned. Part III is an integrative chapter, with a discussion of the findings in this book. Attention is paid to the body of literature on corporate universities, strategic balancing acts that corporate universities have to deal with, and directions for future research and development.

Chapter 2: Strategy Development for Continuous Learning

Every organization needs to find answers to the ultimate strategic challenge of continuous adaptation to stay in tune with the environment. This chapter frames the endeavor of continuous adaptation in a sleek approach based on systems thinking. A case about the development of the Metropolitan Opera in New York City from a local opera house to an international business is used to unveil how strategy and learning come together. The concepts of market system, business system, organizational system, and personal system contribute a complete overview of the most important factors in realizing continuous adjustment. The chapter also discusses the connection between strategic change and learning, introducing the concepts of *learning as usual* and *exceptional learning*. This chapter makes it clear that strategy needs learning:

> Strategy development is about learning what should be done and what can be done.

Chapter 3: Corporate University Strategy

This chapter sheds light on the connections that link corporate university strategy with business strategy. The underlying logic is that corporate universities are supposed to play a significant role in the renewal, implementation, or optimization of strategy in their organizations. At the beginning of the chapter the imperative of continuous alignment, as described in Chapter 2, is combined with the fundamental strategic notion that the long-term success of organizations depends on the ability both to exploit current capabilities and to explore fundamentally new competencies (Raisch et al., 2009). Building on this exploitation–exploration strategy dichotomy (and the need for transformation to move from one to the other), then adding international research outcomes, three generic corporate university strategies are constructed and worked out to reveal their distinctive business system characteristics.[5] The resulting School (exploitation), College (transformation), and Academy (exploration) strategies underpin the development of consistent and focused business systems for corporate universities. As is argued by the author:

> The three generic corporate university strategies offer a conceptual basis on which to assess the current strategic roles of corporate universities in organizations, and to envision their future roles.

Chapter 4: Corporate University Value Creation and Learning Formats

To stay focused, it is important for corporate universities to have a general strategy, but it takes more than that to ensure that organizational learning is heading in the right direction. Corporate university strategies need to be tailored for specific learning needs and opportunities in the organization. The two key questions are: What value does the corporate university need to create? Which learning formats need to be deployed? Two instruments are introduced here to explore those questions in more detail: the Value Creation Menu and the Learning Formats Model. The Value Creation Menu covers choices pertaining to the dimensions of organizational and individual learning, and to value creation achieved by the expansion of competences and relationships. The Learning Formats Model builds upon the work of David Kolb (1984) on experiential learning, and it features an inventory of the most important learning formats seen at corporate universities. The two instruments are applied in-depth to the corporate universities of Ahold (a retail company), Heineken (known for their export beer), and TNT (postal and parcel services). Moreover, a range of international examples are used to highlight the value creation focus of corporate universities in companies such as Kenya Airways, Pertamina, VolkerWessels, IHC Merwede, RWS, CRH, Haniel, Deloitte, Mars, Disney, and Apple. One conclusion drawn in the chapter holds true for all:

> Corporate universities need to make sure that learning hits organization needs. Hence, they constantly need to review their options for value creation and renew their learning formats.

Chapter 5: Mars University: Raising the Bar

The chapter on strategic renewal and transformation at Mars Inc., a private, family-owned company operating in the global food, pet food, and confectionery industries, opens the series of six cases regarding the strategic role of corporate universities. The Mars University case revolves around the interplay between corporate strategy and corporate university evolution, denoted as co-evolution in Figure 1.1.[6] The chapter describes how Mars University has moved from an internationally decentralized ad hoc training operation to a globally unified driver of learning that fulfills the role of a key enabler of strategy. It is safe to say that, along the way, the corporate university has been successful in seizing senior management attention. Mars University is a multi-unit corporate university offering a broad range of programs. One unit that draws special attention is the Customized Learning Group – the innovation arm of the corporate university with the task to address new business challenges that go beyond the learning solutions provided by the Mars University curriculum. The momentum and leadership capability which this corporate university has been building up over almost a decade is increasingly turning organizational learning within Mars from one of support for change to that of a driver of change. Yet, the essence of corporate learning within Mars remains the same. In the words of Jon Shepherd, the former CLO of Mars University, the essence is

> to get a competitive edge, using learning to meet business challenges and provide consistency around the world in an efficient manner.

Chapter 6: Deloitte University: Developing as One

Deloitte is one of the largest professional service firms in the world and it comprises 200,000 professionals working in independent firms located all around the world. Learning and leadership development are considered crucial to making the "As One Strategy" of the company work. With this in mind, Deloitte University (established in 2011 after a US$300 million investment by the US member firms) has transformed learning across the entire Deloitte organization. Virtually all thinkable learning formats are deployed to enable professionals at all levels to connect, share their thoughts, and to identify and capitalize on new ideas and approaches. The curriculum of the university is comprehensive, covering technical, industry, and professional tracks. One of the compelling characteristics of Deloitte University, as described in the chapter, is that program decisions are based on extensive collaboration with large groups of highly autonomous stakeholders throughout the company. It seems that the relatively young corporate university has just begun to realize the full potential of corporate learning for Deloitte. The words of Bill Pelster, the principal of Deloitte Consulting LLP Human Capital practice and former CLO of Deloitte, give an indication of the ambition levels of Deloitte University:

> In the area of corporate learning, I believe the future isn't necessarily about the latest gadgets – though of course technology plays a fundamental role. I think the true revolution is about a much simpler idea – nothing more, nothing less, than a new definition of "learning" itself.[7]

Chapter 7: Shell Project Academy: Developing a Learning Community

The Shell Project Academy has become a source of inspiration for a range of corporate universities within the international oil and gas industry. The lessons learned in establishing the corporate university, however, are relevant to a much broader audience. The Shell Project Academy aims to take the Shell capability in (complex) project management to a world-class level with an accredited program. Project management, a cross-disciplinary function that permeates the entire corporation, is of crucial importance to companies like Shell, as it is a determining factor in obtaining access to new oil and gas reserves in the world. The chapter on the Shell Project Academy describes, quite in detail, why the corporate university was established, the design of a comprehensive program, its costs and performance levels, and the governance structure for balanced "ownership" of the corporate university. Moreover, it is explained how a Project Management Community is built and sustained as a cornerstone of corporate learning. The community is one of the five complementary components of the Shell Project Academy program, also known as the SPA Pentagon. This Pentagon forms a tightly integrated organizational learning system with important synergy effects between the different components. As a Shell official put it:

> Don't try changing the Pentagon into a Square – it would no longer work.

Chapter 8: Canon Academy: Accelerating Transformation

The chapter on Canon Academy in Europe provides a detailed view of the vital role that a corporate university can play in strategy implementation. Canon, the Japanese company primarily known for its cameras, copiers and printers, is in the process of transforming itself into an integrated imaging hardware, software and services company. The Canon Academy is pivotal in cascading the strategy from a corporate level to further specified strategies and their implementation in regional and local markets. Examples from the Canon printing business and the consumer imaging market describe how corporate learning is used to drive strategy implementation. A common thread is that the corporate university brings the relevant people together and engages with them in a process of finding out what the people at Canon need to learn to make a given strategy work. Strategy interpretation, specification, and implementation are part of the process. The corporate university staff members have regular and direct contact with senior management to stay in close touch with the business needs and to drive organizational learning:

> It is not difficult to view the Canon Academy as an instrument for senior management to lead the organization.... We meet on a regular basis to figure out how to enable the people in the organization to actually move in the right direction, and to find out what they need to know to do so.

Chapter 9: Corporate University Strategy Renewal at ING

The lifecycle of the ING Business School (later ING Bank Academy) is captured in this exemplary chapter on corporate university evolution, decline, and possible revival. Attention is paid to the effects of the worldwide financial crisis which took hold in 2008 on corporate learning at ING Group (later ING Bank). The ING Business School lifecycle covers 15 years, including the early years (1998–2002), the era of growth and expansion (2003–8), the turmoil due to the financial crisis (2009–11), and the aftermath up to 2013. The four different eras stand for profound changes in the strategic role of the corporate university in response and anticipation of corporate strategy renewal. One of the changes that does catch the eye is the shift from push (mandatory courses) to a pull (business demand-driven) approach to corporate learning in the expansion era of the corporate university. In the turmoil era, a remarkable shift is made from a stable, course-based approach to short-cycle, customized leadership and implementation projects. Strategic renewal – following a gradual path, but being revolutionary in more recent years – is the common thread of this chapter:

> The way ING Business School transformed into the ING Bank Academy shows how the priority and role of corporate learning in organizations can change quite dramatically in a short timeframe.

Chapter 10: Bringing Speed to Knowledge: A Dean's Journey

This chapter traces the professional life of Stefaan van Hooydonk as a corporate university Dean, covering sixteen years, four countries, and six organizations. That track shows how the corporate universities of Nokia (in China and later also global), Agfa HealthCare, and Philips Lighting have enhanced their strategic impact through new ways to reach economies of scale and scope, getting people to *want to learn* instead of *having to learn* – and, in particular, in the case of Philips Lighting University, the paradigm shift that they have experienced in organizational learning. Special attention is paid to the issue of creating pull and output control with a smart certification system and some time is spent on the question why Philips Lighting University is doing away with its learning management system (LMS) rather than honing it. The chapter also touches on new approaches that were pioneered to make informal learning and performance support work for Philips Lighting, for instance with the creation of "flash communities" of sales people across different geographical regions. One of the insights shared in the chapter points out much of the essence of the Dean's journey:

> advances in digital technology have unlocked the possibility for individuals to take responsibility for their own learning in organizations. To make this work, people in organizations not only need to be provided with flexible access to a range of learning resources, but they also have to be motivated to learn what is relevant to the organization.

Chapter 11: Corporate University Definitions, Literature, and Lessons Learned

The final chapter of this book treats definitions and developments in the corporate university literature. The boundaries of the corporate university concept are explored with examples from two large firms and one small company with global presence: IKEA, FrieslandCampina, and Ducati. Moreover, key lessons are derived from analyzing, comparing, and contrasting the six in-depth cases in the book. The lessons learned cover the deployment of generic strategies, and the issues of strategy specificity, the corporate university profile in the organization, and tracking performance. Finally, an agenda for future research is presented.

Reading tips

The chapters of this book on corporate universities are interconnected with the theme of strategy. Some chapters build upon those which come before them in the particular order of their presentation, but they can be read separately just as well, to satisfy the specific interests of different readers.

- Readers who are curious about what *state-of-the-art business strategy* is about, how it works, or who want to explore the business strategy idiom, may find it best to start with Chapter 2. The concepts of market system, business system, organizational system, and personal system provide a thorough overview of all the ingredients required to shape strategy. This chapter also clarifies the connection between strategy and learning.
- For readers interested in *corporate university strategy formation*, Chapters 3 and 4 provide a good read. The trichotomy of generic school, college, and academy strategies in Chapter 3 supplies the foundation for clear strategic choices when envisioning the future strategic role of a corporate university. The instruments provided in Chapter 4 help to specify corporate university ambitions in terms of value creation for the parent organization, and to select appropriate learning formats.
- Chapters 5 to 10 are recommended as a source of inspiration for readers interested in *real-life cases on the strategic role of corporate universities*. Suggestion: From these chapters, select an organization that closely resembles your own, or piques your interest, and start reading there. You may also enjoy exploring the corporate university of an organization that is quite different from yours.
- For an overview of the most important *insights from this book, a corporate university definition, strategic issues for corporate universities,* and *an agenda for future research,* read Chapter 11.

Why this book

The academic and management literature published on the strategic role of corporate universities in organizations is scarce.[8] In contrast, thousands of corporate universities worldwide form a rich source of research data for scholars, and an important source of experience and *practices worth sharing* for practitioners. It would be a shame if all this were to remain unknown and unshared. As strikingly formulated by Glaser and Marks (1966) already decades ago:[9]

> All over the world people struggle with problems and seek solutions. Often these who struggle are unaware that others face similar problems, and in some instances, are solving them.

This book offers a foundation for leaders, executives, scholars, and advisors to structurally develop, utilize, and share knowledge on the strategic role of corporate universities in organizations.

Notes

1. It is unknown how many corporate universities exist worldwide. There are some indicators, though. For instance, in a relatively small and highly industrialized country like the Netherlands, with close to 17 million inhabitants, over 100 corporate universities are known to be active. In the world's corporate university heartland, USA, with a population totaling more than 300 million, the numbers mentioned by consultants and scholars range from many hundreds to over 1000. Corporate universities have become common in the UK and France, too, and they are becoming more widespread in most industrialized and emerging economies.
2. Source: Steffens and Novotne (2007)
3. The RZD corporate university contributes, among others, to the long-term Development Strategy 2030. Sources: http://eng.rzd.ru and www.makonews.ru/155.html.
4. The early General Electric corporate university (currently known as the John F. Welch Leadership Center, or "Crotonville") opened its doors in 1956 when the company, lacking sufficient numbers of trained managers to diversify and stay competitive, decided to establish its own, in-company management education center.
5. The concept of generic strategy is based on the notion as introduced by Michael Porter (1985).
6. The concept of co-evolution in organizational theory is used to explain adaptive processes of organizations to changes in their environment, and vice versa. In short, industries, organizations and their units develop over time in an ongoing process of mutual adaptation. A fundamental force driving co-evolution is the strategic tension between exploitation and exploration (March, 1991), which is described in more detail in Chapter 3 of this book.
7. Source: Van Dam (2011, ix).
8. See Chapter 11 in this book for an overview of the corporate university literature.
9. This quote has been taken from the PhD thesis by Peter Boone (1997), as the original source appears no longer accessible.

Literature

Boone, P.F. (1997). *Managing Intracorporate Knowledge Sharing.* PhD thesis. Rotterdam: Eburon.
Dam, N. Van (2011). *Next Learning Unwrapped.* Raleigh, NC: Lulu Publishers.
Glaser, E.M., and J.B. Marks (1966). Putting Research to Work. *Rehabilitation Record,* Vol. 7, No. 6, pp. 6–10.
Kolb, D.A. (1984). *Experiential Learning: Experience as the source of learning and development.* Englewood Cliffs, NJ: Prentice-Hall.
March, J. (1991). Exploration and Exploitation in Organizational Learning. *Organization Science,* Vol. 2, No. 2, pp. 71–87.
Porter, M. (1985). *Competitive Advantage: Creating and Sustaining Superior Performance.* New York: The Free Press.
Raisch, S., J. Birkinshaw, G. Probst, M.L. Tushman (2009). Organizational Ambidexterity: Balancing Exploitation and Exploration for Sustained Performance. *Organization Science,* Vol. 20, No. 4, pp. 685–95.
Steffens, L.E., and S.M. Novotne (2007). Corporate Universities in Small Companies. In: M. Allen (ed.) *The Next Generation of Corporate Universities: Innovative Approaches for Developing People and Expanding Organizational Capabilities.* San Francisco: Pfeiffer.

2
STRATEGY DEVELOPMENT FOR CONTINUOUS LEARNING

Guest author: Ron Meyer

> New opinions are always suspected, and usually opposed, without any other reason but because they are not already common.
>
> —*John Locke*

When Peter Gelb became head of New York's famous Metropolitan Opera in 2006, he quickly realized that in the 120 years of its existence very little had changed. Since its founding in 1883 by such prominent families as the Vanderbilts, Astors, and Roosevelts, "the Met" had staged extravagant operas, selling tickets to the New York elite and enticing them to donate large sums of money. Yet, while the Met remained a bastion of conservative taste, the outside music scene had kept on changing, first slowly, but picking up speed as Elvis, the Beatles, and Motown happened. To his dismay, Gelb saw that the average age of his audience had passed 65 and that the number of young visitors had dwindled to a mere handful. At the same time, patrons had shifted their generosity to more modern charities, such as medical research and environmental protection, while sponsors had switched to sports and other large-scale entertainment events. The result had been that for years the Met had been running a large deficit and that there was no end in sight to the financial free fall. Yet, despite this bleak budgetary situation, the powerful local unions were set to block any form of modernization.

Gelb, who was not an opera-world insider but the former head of the US music division of Sony, started a metamorphosis. To appeal to a younger audience, he expanded the repertoire to include operas with more drama and action, while simultaneously developing special marketing campaigns to target this "MTV generation." He also opened up rehearsals to the public and displayed the opening nights on a large screen at the Lincoln Center. But his biggest innovation was to beam performances live by satellite to thousands of movie theaters around the world, enlarging the Met's audience from tens of thousands to millions.

To achieve this, Gelb had to convince the unions to jump from a nineteenth-century craftsman approach to a twenty-first-century multimedia set up, with 15 cameras, 60 extra technicians and TV people taking over production (De Wit and Meyer, 2010).

The strategic challenge: continuous alignment

This story about Gelb and the Metropolitan Opera is a "dramatic" illustration of the most important challenge facing all organizations, namely remaining aligned with the changing outside world. Even in very stable and conservative environments, such as the opera scene, change happens and even the mighty must adapt themselves to the unfolding circumstances. For organizations, the same Darwinist principle is true as for organisms – it's all about "survival of the fittest." The one who best fits the shifting conditions in the environment will survive, while the others will only be found in the fossil records.

More dramatic staging to appeal to a younger audience and broadcasting operas to movie theaters are two examples of adapting the business system of the Metropolitan Opera to the new market circumstances. The business system is literally the way in which an organization conducts its business. It is the manner in which a firm creates value for a selected part of the market. In Figure 2.1 this alignment between the business system and the market system is captured in a conceptual model (Meyer, 2007).

The top layer of the business system is the value proposition – that which the organization presents to potential buyers, hoping they will judge it to be valuable. This is more than only a product or service. A value proposition is a bundle of attributes that reinforce each other and together create value for the buyer. So, while the Met sells tickets to an opera, its value proposition includes comfortable chairs, explanation about the opera, an elegant environment, a social circuit, and high status.

To be able to market the new value proposition, Gelb also needed to change the way in which the value proposition was created. He had to adapt many of the value-adding activities such as the Met's way of marketing, its approach to sales and the whole manner in which productions were staged. This is the middle part of the business system. Besides these primary value-adding activities, Gelb also had to adjust many support activities such as human resource management, IT, and facility management. Because all of these value-adding activities need to be aligned and linked to each other, the whole value-adding activity system is referred to as the value chain (Porter, 1985).

The bottom layer of the business system is composed of the resources that are used as inputs for the value chain. The Met, for instance, has many tangible resources, such as buildings, sets, musical instruments, and new broadcasting equipment, but more importantly many intangible resources, such as its reputation, relationships, knowledge, and competencies. Here, too, Gelb needed to drive renewal, as the Met had limited "relational capital" among the younger public and no broadcasting know-how.

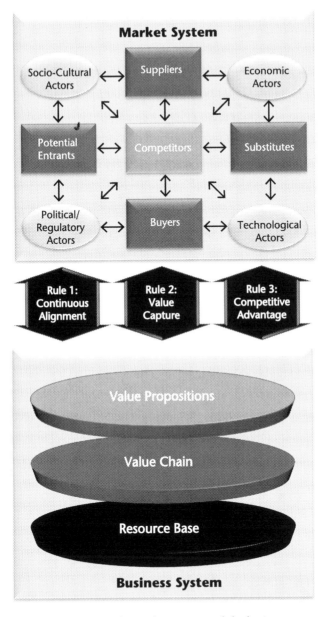

FIGURE 2.1 Aligning the market system and the business system
Source: Analysis by the author

If these three layers of the business system are well-aligned and the business system itself is well-aligned with the market system, then the first requirement for strategic success will have been met – *Rule #1: "Ensure business alignment."* However, there are two more basic rules that need to be obeyed to be successful:

Rule #2 is "Ensure value capture" – make sure that buyers actually pay for the value they receive. If a firm supplies valuable products and/or services to its clients, but these clients aren't willing to pay sufficiently for the value created, this business system will not be viable in the long run. Facebook and Skype are examples of companies creating value for their customers, but without being paid enough to cover the costs. An often-used solution to this problem is to search for a secondary customer group (besides the users) for whom value can also be created, such as advertisers or sponsors, and who are willing to pay. This is referred to as an alternative "cost and revenue model" – a way of tapping in to multiple income streams to cover operating expenses.

Rule #3 is "Ensure competitive advantage" – make sure that the business system is better than that of alternative providers, so buyers will have a strong preference and competition will be less price-oriented, or the price competition can be won. Obviously a competitive advantage that is sustainable for a longer period of time is better than one that can be quickly eroded by rivals, so most companies will strive to find a competitive advantage that is based on more than only a differentiated product. Developing a differentiated value proposition, or even better, a differentiated business system, generally makes it much more difficult to beat or imitate. A business system based on different principles than those of its competitors is referred to as having a distinctive underlying "business model."

It is important to note that alignment goes both ways. Often firms need to adapt to changes in market circumstances, but firms can also be the drivers of market change. The market didn't force Gelb to broadcast operas to thousands of theaters; he initiated the change. In this instance, he wasn't a "rule taker" but a "rule maker," not following external demands, but shaping them. The result was a two-way alignment process between the market system and the business system of the Met, often referred to as co-evolution.

Continuous alignment between business and organization

But the Met is more than only the opera business – it is also a group of people working together in a systematic way to be able to stage operas. In other words, to be able to make the business system function, the Met has a supporting organizational system. While the business system is about production (using inputs to create outputs), the organizational system is about people. These two systems also need to be continuously aligned with one another (see Figure 2.2).

The most direct link is between the business system and the formal organization, that is, the organization as officially designed on paper. So, for example, Gelb's

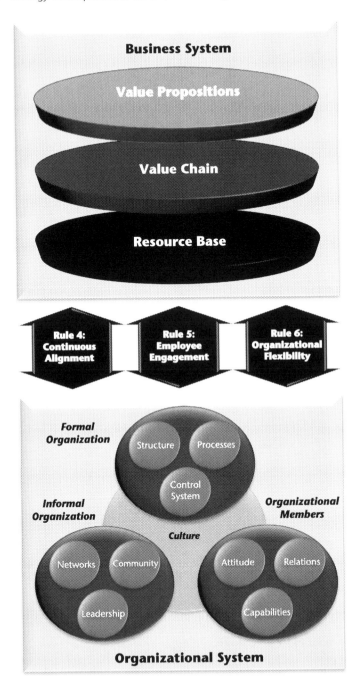

FIGURE 2.2 Alignment between business system and organizational system

Source: Analysis by the author

decision to direct more marketing activities at a younger audience led to the formation of a separate marketing team (change of organizational structure), close cooperation between this team and the unit responsible for opera programming (change of organizational processes), and stricter directing of both units by Gelb himself (change of control system). As can be derived from this example, an organizational structure is the way in which value-adding activities have been divided between units and individuals (division of labor/task differentiation), while organizational processes are the means by which the various value-adding activities are coordinated and linked together again into a consistent whole (coordination of labor/task integration). The control system is the means by which units and individuals are monitored and steered.

But an organization is more than only its design. To a large extent the functioning of an organization is determined by the people populating the structure. The capabilities, relational networks, and attitudes of the members of the organization will have a huge influence on how the organizational design is brought to life. So, when realigning an organizational system to a changing business system, one must go much further than only redrawing org charts. People might need to be trained to upgrade their skills, they can be brought into contact with key stakeholders to strengthen their relational networks, and they can be coached to change their attitudes. And where necessary organizational members can be replaced by more suitable candidates.

The third key aspect of an organizational system is its informal side, which are all characteristics that have emerged along the way, without being explicitly designed. For example, in every organization informal networks between people grow, facilitating information exchange, aiding the coordination of activities, shaping ideas, influencing decision-making, sharing rumors, and helping each other out. These networks can be counterproductive and undermine formal channels, but on the other hand they are generally crucial for working together in a flexible way. Cooperation requires people to know, trust, involve, correct, and compromise with one another, and nowhere in the formal organization is this taken care of. Cooperation emerges spontaneously within networks that sometimes follow the lines of the formal organization, but often develop following a different logic.

Leadership is also informal, as leaders are not appointed, but step up and are accepted as such. Some formally appointed managers will exhibit leadership behavior and thus can have significant impact on the functioning of the organization, but having a formal position of power doesn't necessarily ensure they will be embraced as leaders. Sometimes, it is actually people without a formal management position that have informal authority, allowing them to play an important role in adapting the organizational system to the business system. This was also true at the Met, where a few old hands wielded enormous informal power, and it was their support that helped Gelb to achieve his envisioned transformation.

A sense of community within an organization can also not be designed, but can only be influenced to grow. A spirit of involvement, connectedness, and loyalty can be encouraged and cherished, but it takes time to take root and flourish. For

Gelb, it was actually this strong team spirit and devotion to the institution that was the starting point for change, as employees were willing to make personal sacrifices and endure uncertainty to the benefit of the larger whole.

The intangible result of these three main elements – the formal organization, the organizational members, and the informal organization – is the organizational culture. A culture is a joint worldview and shared values, on which unwritten behavioral rules ("norms") are based. Culture can't be directly shaped, but can only be indirectly influenced via the other three main elements of the organizational system.

If all four main elements of the organizational system are well-aligned, and the organizational system is in turn well-aligned to the business system, then the fourth requirement for strategic success will have been met – *Rule #4: "Ensure organizational alignment."* However, there are two more rules that need to be obeyed to be successful:

Rule #5 is "Ensure employee engagement" – make sure that employees are not only able, but also willing. Of course, organizations need to have the capability to run the business system effectively and efficiently, but without team spirit the result will always remain suboptimal. The difference between a sports team that is good and one that is great is usually not found in a difference of individual capabilities, but in their motivation to play as a team. The organizational system must therefore not only be trained to be a strong "body," but must also have "spirit" breathed into it.

Rule #6 is "Ensure organizational flexibility" – make sure the organizational system is not too specifically tailored to the current business system, as this will build in future rigidity. If the organization is too narrowly focused on one particular business model, much as the panda can only eat bamboo, it will be too vulnerable if continuous alignment is required. Flexibility can be found in, for example, people, processes, and a culture that can function in a variety of circumstances (flexibility through broad organizational suitability), but also in the ability to learn and change quickly (flexibility through high organizational agility).

Here, too, it might seem that the organizational system must always be adapted to the envisioned business system. However, the alignment can go both ways, whereby sometimes a new business model is chosen because it fits well with the strengths of the existing organization. This is why Gelb purposely did not choose to broaden the Met's repertoire to include musicals to attract the younger audience. Branching out into the musical business would have totally clashed with the Met's organizational system, requiring hardnosed organizational changes and a likely loss of employee engagement. On the other hand, broadcasting operas to the entire world is in line with the key strength of the Met's organization system to stage world-class opera performances, requiring only limited new broadcasting capabilities to be learned.

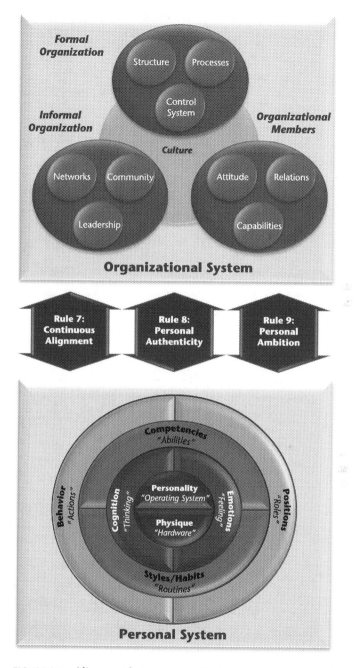

FIGURE 2.3 Alignment between organization system and personal system
Source: Analysis by the author

Continuous alignment between organization and individuals

Not only organizations need to adapt to changing business needs, but so do the individuals in organizations. They, too, must continuously learn and adjust to new demands. In Figure 2.3 this pressure to adapt the personal system of each individual to the unfolding organizational system is summarized in a conceptual model.

There are many ways to simplify complex people into a model, but here the aspects of the individual that are most important for organizational success have been selected and grouped into four rings. The outer ring consists of behavior and positions. Behavior is what individuals do and positions are the formal and informal roles that people play, for example, the formal position of sales manager and the informal position of social media opinion leader. Behavior and positions are relatively easy for other people to see and relatively easy for a person to change.

Both behavior and positions are fed by the deeper layer of competencies and habits. Competencies are the abilities that an individual has learnt to master, while habits are the routines that an individual develops by continuously doing things in a particular way (a collection of habits is often referred to as a style). To be able to recognize a person's competencies and/or habits requires a bit more effort, while changing them also requires a bit more effort by the person involved.

The drivers of how competencies and habits are developed and deployed are found at the next level down. These are the way people think (cognition) and feel (emotions). People's patterns of thought are much more deeply engrained than commonly assumed, as they are based on a well-developed picture of how the world functions, referred to as a cognitive map, and tend to follow standard forms of reasoning, referred to as cognitive scripts. People's emotions, varying from fear to love, are also deeply embedded in an individual's psyche, sometimes bypassing a person's conscious thought, sometimes shaping it. Both thinking and feeling are much more difficult to perceive than the outer two rings and equally difficult to change.

At the core of an individual are the elements that are more or less immutable, namely the physical hardware of a person (including their genetic code) and their personality structure. And not only is this level unchangeable, it is also extremely difficult to recognize what is going on at this level.

If all levels of the personal system are well-aligned to each other and in turn the personal system is well-aligned to the organizational system, then the seventh requirement for strategic success will have been met – *Rule #7: "Ensure personal alignment."* But here, too, there are two additional rules that need to be obeyed.

Rule #8 is "Ensure personal authenticity" – make sure that in adapting to the organizational system you don't alienate yourself from your own core. When the organization changes, or a person changes positions within the organization, it is usually necessary to adjust behaviors, competencies, and routines. But if these changes are at odds with the level of cognition and emotions, this can be disorienting and dissatisfying. Too much "stretch" between the levels leads to stress. The solution can sometimes be found in, literally, "changing your mind," but one can also look for a style that fits better with the inner rings or for a different position.

Rule #9 is "Ensure alignment with personal ambitions" – make sure that in adaping to the organizational system you keep your personal objectives clearly in mind. If a person has the ambition to move to other positions within the organization, it will be necessary to develop accordingly. But alignment goes both ways, so it can also be an ambition to change the organization. Of course, individuals can also have personal development ambitions, but also social ambitions, such as having more time for family, friends and/or the broader community. Whichever ambitions one has, they need to be aligned and in balance with each other, and together determine in which way the personal system will be aligned to the organizational system.

Forms of continuous learning

In Figure 2.4, all of the aforementioned alignment relationships are brought together in one model. In practice, people in organizations experience these alignment efforts in three main ways, which are illustrated by the three types of numbered arrows.

The most common way that people encounter the need for alignment is in their daily work. Every individual is constantly learning how to work optimally within the existing organization. Even the most talented people can still find ways to improve themselves and achieve a higher performance within a stable organizational system. And as people often progress to new positions, there is a continuous need to learn new behaviors, develop new competencies, and establish new routines. This type of *learning as usual* is called *people development*, or more specifically management development, when referring to organizational members in a management position. All organizations need to ensure that such learning takes place, as will be seen in later chapters of this book.

In the case of strategic change, there is much more alignment going on. Not only the two bottom systems in Figure 2.4 need to be adjusted to one another, but all four systems need to be aligned. People in the organization notice that they need to adapt because changes in the market system make it necessary. It is no longer about learning as usual within a stable organizational system, but *exceptional learning* – acquiring new insights, skills, routines, and behaviors that help to reestablish the fit between the market, the business and the organizational system.

Organizational members can experience this realignment process in two different ways, depending on their participation in creating the strategic response to the market challenges. If a person is not involved in strategy development, but only in *strategy implementation*, then the alignment will go from top to bottom – because the market has changed, the business system has been adapted, requiring the

20 Strategy Development for Continuous Learning

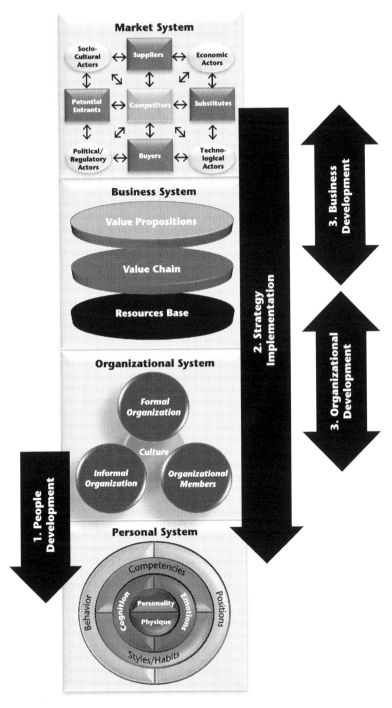

FIGURE 2.4 Forms of continuous learning

Source: Analysis by the Author

organization to be adjusted, making it necessary for the individual to learn new behaviors. This type of exceptional learning by people in the organization, which is required for successful strategy implementation, is called *transformational learning*. It is all about the question: "How do I need to change to fit in the new strategy?"

For people who are involved in strategy development, the learning process is entirely different. They are not primarily concerned with their personal alignment to the altered strategy, but rather in shaping the alignment between the top three systems. If they are involved in realigning the market system and the business system, they are engaged in *business development* – exploring ways to improve how value is created for potential clients. If they are involved in realigning the business system and the organizational system, they are engaged in *organizational development* – exploring ways to get the organizational members to work together as optimally as possible. In both cases, the type of exceptional learning required is called *explorational learning*, as the knowledge which people want to acquire still needs to be found and/or created.

Strategy implementation as a continuous learning process

The term "strategy implementation" suggests a simple process of execution. Doing what is stated in the strategic plan. Yet, in reality, strategic plans are hardly ever detailed blueprints that can be mindlessly followed. It is not merely "painting by numbers." Strategy implementation requires quite a bit of interpretation of the big picture outlined and a considerable amount of filling in the blanks.

Strategic plans that need to be implemented can actually vary wildly in the amount of detail they provide, as outlined in Figure 2.5. At the most specific level, strategic plans can indeed offer a blueprint, leaving little to the discretion of the implementers. In such a strategic blueprint all the necessary changes to the business system and organizational system will have been worked out into the smallest detail, requiring organization members to simply "follow the recipe."

Slightly less comprehensively detailed is a strategic roadmap, while a strategic framework only outlines the main elements of the strategy, clarifying the key objectives and initiatives that need to be undertaken. Strategic guidelines are even more broadly defined, offering a number of objectives, principles, and preferences that give general direction to where the firm ought to be headed. A strategic vision, finally, is even less specific on what needs to be done, as it only paints a rough sketch of a desired long-term future.

At all five levels one can speak of a strategy – a selected course of action to achieve the overall purpose of the organization. Yet, the lower the level of detail of the strategy, the more that strategy implementation will mean filling in those details along the way. Mere strategy execution will start to include more experimentation and exploration. Within the outline provided by the strategy, people will need to be engaged in business development and organizational development. This makes the early distinction between strategy implementation and strategy development less clear-cut in reality.

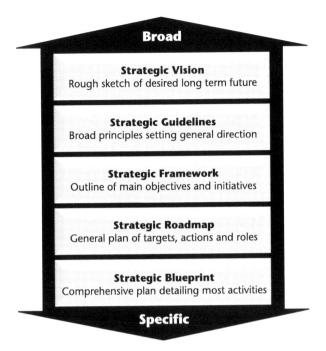

FIGURE 2.5 Levels of strategy specificity
Source: Author's analysis

Due to the increasing unpredictability of markets and the rising complexity of organizations, the trend is actually towards less detailed strategic plans. There is often a preference to get moving and let things emerge, instead of trying to work out everything into roadmaps or blueprints before moving into action. The trend is from "figuring out upfront" to "finding out along the way," which means that people need to discover, not only deploy. This requires organizational members to actively think on their feet, deal with the uncertainty of not having an instruction manual, and to continuously learn as the strategy unfolds.

Even where the strategy has been meticulously specified in a roadmap or blueprint, it is increasingly important that employees don't blindly implement, but critically consider whether the detailed activities make sense and are consistent with the strategic framework. Moreover, they need to remain alert whether the strategic actions have not been made redundant by the rapid changes happening in the market. The need for "foot soldiers," who unquestioningly follow orders, has been superseded by the need for "special forces," who knowing their "commander's intent," have the ability to adapt their approach to volatile, uncertain, complex, and ambiguous conditions. Employees shouldn't only be organized by strategic plans, but should also have the ability to self-organize and adapt the plans. Implementation ain't what it used to be.

Business development as a continuous learning process

When speaking of business development – the alignment of the business system with the market system – it is important to make a distinction between *business optimization* and *business innovation*. Business optimization is a form of business development whereby alignment is sought on the basis of the existing business model. It is also referred to as *exploitation*, as the investments in the existing value chain and resource base are utilized as much as possible, focusing on incremental changes to remain aligned with the market system. Business innovation, on the other hand, is about finding new ways of creating value outside of the existing business model. It is about doing things differently than before, often in ways that are new to the industry or even new to the world. As discovering such new value propositions and value chains requires quite a bit of scouting and experimentation, business innovation is also referred to as *exploration* (March, 1991).

In general, business optimization is easier to plan in more detail than business innovation, as the rules of the game in the market are better known and there is more experience in running the existing business system. Innovation, on the other hand, is per definition a learning process. The only certainty is how little one knows for certain – what could the value proposition look like, how will potential buyers react, which rules of the competitive game can be rewritten and how should the value chain be structured? With this many unknowns one can only feel one's way through the murky mists of the future and accept that exploration demands learning by doing and slow stepwise progress. Setting a detailed roadmap and driving at high speed through the mist is only for the thrill-seekers.

For both business optimization and business innovation it is not a good idea to limit strategy development to only a small group within the organization. Ideas for optimization and innovation are not the preserve of specific individuals or departments, but can emerge anywhere, especially if employees are explicitly asked to think about ways of retaining alignment with the market system. While innovation used to be the domain of R&D departments, increasingly innovations are coming from all different parts of the organization, and even from cooperation with external partners, which is called open innovation. Business optimization, too, is not beholden to only the marketing department, but can benefit from the joint intelligence of the entire organization, if all organizational members are involved in the strategy development process.

Conclusions

Fundamentally, strategy is about the continuous alignment of the business and organizational systems with the market system. A strategy can remain broadly consistent for years, but at a more detailed level even a consistent strategy is always in flux. Adaptations are continuously required to react to external changes, while new initiatives never turn out as expected, requiring corrective action. Hence, strategy development is about finding out what must be done, but also what can be done.

Strategy development is a continuous learning process because the future is so difficult to predict. How will consumers behave in future, how will technologies change, how will the economy develop, which political crises await us, which acquisition will upset the power balance in our industry, which new entrant will suddenly change the rules of the competitive game? Even the most advanced trend watchers do little better than your average weather service. The future is unknowable and therefore any strategy will be based on assumptions about the future, of which we will only learn along the way which were correct.

Yet learning is not only reactively discovering what must be done under pressure of market changes, but it is also proactively finding out what can be done. By experimenting with new business models one can find out where the rules of the competitive game can be changed. By launching innovative value propositions one can find out how consumer taste can be shaped. And one can bet on various horses at the same time, to see where the market is pliable and where it is immutable.

This continuous learning process shouldn't simply be dropped on the desk of the CEO, the strategy department or external consultants. The best results are achieved if the alignment between the business and the market is an organization-wide responsibility. Broad participation in strategy development not only leads to more business development ideas, but also to more acceptance and support to realize the necessary organizational and personal changes.

Literature

De Wit, B. and R.J.H. Meyer (2010). *Strategy Synthesis: Resolving Strategy Paradoxes to Create Competitive Advantage*, 3rd edition. London: Cengage.

March, J. (1991). Exploration and Exploitation in Organizational Learning. *Organization Science*, Vol. 2, No. 2, pp. 71–87.

Meyer, R.J.H. (2007). *Mapping the Mind of the Strategist: A Quantitative Methodology for Measuring the Strategic Beliefs of Executives*. Rotterdam: ERIM.

Porter, M.E. (1985). *Competitive Advantage: Creating and Sustaining Superior Performance*. New York: Free Press.

3
CORPORATE UNIVERSITY STRATEGY

> What we want to learn, we discover
> especially while learning
> *—Malcolm S. Knowles*

Corporate universities need to know which strategies they should follow to contribute to the competitive strength of their organizations. In other words, how should the corporate university business system[1] be shaped (or re-shaped) to serve the strategic needs of the organization? How to align with strategies that are predominantly exploitative, explorative, or transformational in nature?

For strategy development, many organizations adhere to (variations of) generic strategies that can be found in the management literature.[2] The *Cost Leadership*, *Differentiation*, and *Focus* strategies introduced by Michael Porter (1980, 1985) have become household names among past and present generations of managers. The same is true for the three generic strategies *Operational Excellence*, *Product Leadership*, and *Customer Intimacy* described by Michael Treacy and Fred Wiersema (1995). Generic strategies are relevant instruments for corporate university strategy development, too. After all, corporate universities can be treated as business units serving market needs (i.e., the needs of the organization they serve). Three generic strategies – depicting distinctive corporate university business systems – have become known as *School*, *College*, and *Academy*. The School strategy aims to optimize strategy through corporate learning, College focuses on strategy implementation, and Academy drives strategic renewal.

The three generic corporate university strategies offer a conceptual basis on which to assess the current strategic roles of corporate universities in organizations, and to envision their future roles. One of the most difficult accomplishments for corporate university leaders, executives, and teams who are working on their strategies can be expressed in a single word: focus. As will be argued in this chapter, trying to pursue fully-fledged School, College, and Academy strategies all at the same time evokes tensions, due to incompatible demands for corporate university propositions, processes and resources. Losing strategic focus is likely to lead to suboptimal results, missed opportunities, and the risk of appearing on the senior management radar screen as a candidate for cost cutting.

Just like their parent organizations, corporate universities need a robust and focused strategy in order to excel. The generic School, College, and Academy strategies provide the concepts and language to do just that. They are discussed in greater detail below, taking the fundamental strategic dichotomy of exploitation and exploration as the point of departure.

Exploitation and exploration

For organizations to stay attuned to their environments in the long run, they need to strike a balance between the pressures of having to exploit (utilizing and optimizing the current method of value creation) and to explore (seeking and developing new ways to create *and* capture value). For example, oil companies will do almost anything to optimize the use of their current oil sources: it is all about *exploitation*. At the same time, however, they must continuously search for new oil reserves before the old ones run dry: that is *exploration*. Raisch et al. (2009), in their article on organizational ambidexterity,[3] point out the strategic challenge for organizations to exploit and explore at the same time:

> An organization's long-term success depends on its ability to exploit its current capabilities while simultaneously exploring fundamentally new competencies.

The difficulty is that pursuing an exploitation strategy is a very different ballgame than exploration, with contrasting priorities (stability versus change), leadership styles (executive versus entrepreneurial leadership), structures (solid versus fluid), systems (planning and control versus innovation and development), and outcomes (predictable versus unknown).

Exploitation and exploration are opposites – they form fundamental strategic polarity, as depicted in Figure 3.1. Hence, efforts to enhance an exploration strategy easily conflict with attempts to get more by exploiting the current business system. The ultimate challenge for strategists is to find syntheses between the two strategies, rather than trade-offs, to secure the continuity of the organization.

In the international strategic management literature, the fundamental tensions between strategies for exploitation and exploration can be found, for example, in the works of Chan Kim and René Mauborgne (2005). They argue that organizations should build and adopt a *blue ocean strategy* (where blue ocean stands for an ocean without sharks – a metaphor for markets without competitors). This involves constantly seeking and capturing new markets and the ability to do this faster than rivals. The underlying idea is that an uncultivated market will present still rather

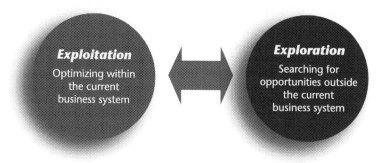

FIGURE 3.1 Exploitation versus exploration
Source: Center for Strategy & Leadership

powerless competitors or none at all. The weaker the competition, the easier it is for companies to achieve above-average margins or, for institutions and non-profit organizations, to enhance their societal impact. *Red ocean strategies*, by contrast, are a necessary evil for the unfortunate organizations that are not able to move out of their competition-ridden red oceans and head into blue water. According to Kim and Mauborgne, competing in red oceans is the fate of organizations that have failed to successfully explore new business models. In tune, strategists like the influential tandem Roger Martin and Alan Lafley consider exploitation expressed in the attitude, *"We can just keep doing what we're already doing"* to be a status quo that *". . . is sometimes a path to decline"* (Lafley et al., 2012: 59–60).

Both in practice and academia, the consensus is that organizations in free-market economies need to reap fruits from exploiting what they have, but that few can afford to refrain from some degree of exploration to identify and take advantage of serving yet-undiscovered or underserved needs in their environment. Having said this, it must be kept in mind that different industries have different strategic time horizons. Industries with relatively long time horizons, such as bulk chemistry or passenger jet manufacturing, are likely to be dominated by companies leaning toward an exploitation strategy.[4] Many companies in the enterprise and gaming software industry, by contrast, tend to favor exploration over exploitation and frequently find themselves in new rounds of transformation. It is not only the environment that determines what they do, however. Organizations can have the capability to shape their environments, too. In the end, balancing exploitation and exploration to secure continuity of the organization in the long run takes sound analysis and judgment on the part of those who are leading the organization.

Three strategy-learning clusters

It is important that corporate university leaders know whether the strategy of the organization is predominantly exploitative or explorative in nature. The nature of the strategy should be taken into account in the configuration of the corporate university business system. After all, an organization with a strategy that emphasizes exploitation has different learning needs than one with an explorative strategy. In Chapter 2 of this book, Ron Meyer links this idea to the terms *learning as usual* (exploitation) and *exceptional learning* (exploration). In practice, learning as usual is found in corporate universities in the shape of program curricula and course catalogues, either accessible via portals for e-learning or in classroom setups, whereby knowledge transfer is the name of the game. By contrast, exceptional learning takes many different shapes and revolves around new knowledge creation – new to the organization at least. Examples include programs that bring people together from different parts and disciplines across the organization, and programs created in cooperation with business school experts to challenge conventional thinking. Their common denominator is the aim to explore and develop new business systems that enable the organization to follow new trends in the environment or to create them.

For corporate universities, there is one more strategic dimension that we must take into account: between exploitation and exploration lies *transformation*, and transformation also lies between exploration and renewed exploitation. Shifting from exploitation to exploration requires a major shift in the mind-set of organizational members: think different, learn different things.[5] Next, a rejuvenated strategy (the outcome of exploration) must first be *implemented* (transformation) before an organization can gain an advantage from it (exploitation). Generally speaking, transformation means that there is still much to be learned to make a new business model work. The implementation of a new strategy goes hand in hand with changes in the organization, including the development of new competencies, systems, and leadership styles. This also requires *exceptional learning*, albeit along the lines of "How to align my unit with the new strategy?" and "What do I need to learn to be effective in the new strategic reality?" These are the questions that underpin the leadership and change programs aiming for organizational and personal development in the light of a new strategy. This form of learning is also called *transformational learning* (Senge, 1990).

In short, exploitation, implementation, and exploration strategies involve fundamentally different learning models: learning as usual, transformational learning, and exceptional learning, respectively. These three tandems of strategy and learning (referred to as strategy-learning clusters) form the conceptual foundation for three generic corporate university strategies.

School, College, and Academy types

Comparing and contrasting the strategic role of a variety of corporate universities from different countries, industries and organizations has resulted in the identification of three general corporate university types, labeled as School, College, and Academy (Rademakers, 2001; 2005). They are considered as Weberian[6] ideal-types (just as the concept of "bureaucracy" is a Weberian ideal-type). Aronovitch (2011) explains what ideal-types (can) do, and what they are not, in just two compact sentences:

> [The ideal-type] insightfully addresses explanatory issues in social science by encompassing the agents' subjective understanding and the need for theorists to comprehend, explain, and evaluate it. As such, ideal-types are not versions of established models in natural science or economics.

The School, College, and Academy types have been constructed to approximate reality with regard to the strategic functions of corporate universities, and with the intention to discuss and investigate corporate universities in a systematic way. In short, the School type represents an efficient design of reactive, strategy-driven learning in organizations, the Academy type is for pro-active knowledge innovation, and the College type is a hybrid form that bridges innovation and optimization.

Organizations tend to treat their corporate universities as business units, which comes with the need for a clear and robust corporate university strategy. A frame of reference that provides a grip on the complexity of strategy formation is helpful in this regard. Generic strategies are such frames of reference. Linking the three corporate university types of School, College, and Academy to the primal forms of strategy (exploitation, transformation, and exploration) and the accompanying learning needs (learning as usual, transformational learning, and exceptional learning) makes it possible to define three generic corporate university strategies: the exploitation-driven school, transformation-driven college, and the exploration-driven academy. The *business system* concept from the strategy literature (Meyer, 2007) forms an academically sound and practical basis to further work out the key characteristics of these three corporate university strategies.[7] The resulting three generic corporate university strategies are mutually exclusive and collectively exhaustive, and provided with the accompanying business system characteristics. The business systems and their characteristics – actually constituting the three generic corporate university strategies – are shown in Table 3.1. In addition, Figure 3.2 captures the connection between the School, College, and Academy strategies and the primal forms of organizational strategy.

An example of a corporate university with an impactful School strategy is Achmea Academy. It is the corporate university of a leading insurance company in the Benelux,[8] pursuing a School strategy under the motto "From craftsmanship to trust." The corporate university contributes, upon direct request of the board of directors, to the ambition of the company to be the most trusted insurance company in the market, a business model that does not undergo significant change. Taking craftsmanship and the right attitude in insurance to the highest possible level in an increasingly complex world of finance defines the essence of the learning services offered.

The Alliantie Academie, the corporate university of a non-profit organization called *De Alliantie*,[9] provides a College strategy example.[10] De Alliantie is a housing corporation that possesses almost 60,000 houses and accommodates approximately

TABLE 3.1 School, College, and Academy business system characteristics

Corporate University business system characteristics		–School– Follow strategy	–College– Implement strategy	–Academy– Renew strategy
Value propositions	Focus	Optimizing current strategy through corporate learning	Strategic transformation through corporate learning	Strategy renewal by boosting knowledge innovation
	Characteristic shape	Catalog with trainings and courses	Programs for organizational development	Pipeline for business system innovations
	Knowledge type	New to the individual	New to the organization	New to the trade
Value chain	Focus	Translating optimized strategy into learning needs for people in the organization	Connecting new strategy to needs for organizational development	Attuning market needs and organizational strength: inside-out; outside-in
	Primary process	Designing, optimizing, and executing corporate curricula	Designing, testing, and executing programs for organizational development	Breaking down barriers for knowledge to flow within and between units and organizations
	Knowledge process	Making relevant knowledge available in a structural way, also maintaining and strengthening it	Managing projects to identify, gather, and deploy the required internal and external knowledge	Driving new knowledge creation by enabling people to meet, share and experiment
Strategic resources	Focus	Deeply understanding the current strategy	Deeply understanding the new strategy	Understanding internal and external developments
	Attitude	Managers – executive leadership style	Intermediaries – facilitative leadership style	Leaders – entrepreneurial leadership style
	Distinctive knowledge	Expertise in the area of educating organizational members	Expertise in the area of organizational development	Expertise in the area of strategy formation and renewal

Source: Analysis by the author

130,000 people in the Netherlands. The college strategy of the corporate university is reflected in the role it has to help the organization digest the merger of three housing corporations into De Alliantie. The corporate university is at the heart of the organization, and it contributes, upon request by senior management, primarily to organizational development in order to take the housing corporation from "Organization version 1.0 to 2.0 and 3.0." Seen from a strategic perspective, the corporate university helps the organization to reap the benefits of synergy and organizational integration through learning programs.

An Academy strategy example is provided by DHV University, part of the global engineering company DHV, which is active in 35 countries around the world.[11] In 2010 the corporate university played a key role when top management launched the initiative to explore, co-develop, and implement a new corporate strategy. A management development program was built to function as a vehicle for strategic renewal. In essence, the corporate university created the circumstances in which the company could take advantage of the deep business knowledge scattered across the organization, and to build support for strategic renewal along the way. In short, a setting was created where learning informed business decisions to realize strategic renewal.[12] During the multi-module program, knowledge started to flow freely and easily, and above all informally, among senior business managers from DHV units operating in different industries and countries around the world. At a first glance, the program seems to resemble any other management development

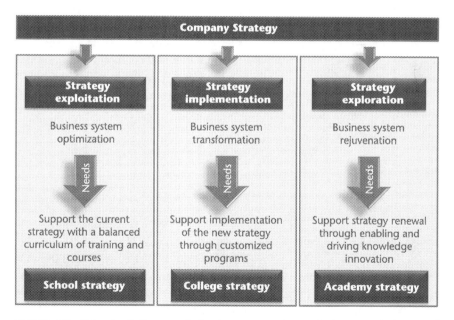

FIGURE 3.2 School, College, and Academy strategies and the primal forms of organizational strategy

Source: Analysis by the author

initiative. A closer look, however, reveals an extensive corporate university value proposition driving strategic renewal.

The generic School, College, and Academy strategies help corporate universities to map out their strategic alternatives that, at the end of the day, should enhance the performance of the organizations they serve. The inherent tensions between the three forms of strategy shed light on the consequences of choosing one strategy over the other or seeking to combine them. In addition, the generic strategies provide a common frame of reference for corporate university leaders who like to exchange thoughts with peers for mutual learning, inspiration, and the identification of practices worth sharing.

The greatest danger of working with generic strategies falls into the category of "unintended usage" – just like using a screwdriver as a crowbar or chisel. It might work to some degree, but inevitably both the tool and the treated object will be damaged. In particular, practitioners and scholars should refrain from mechanistically trying to pigeon-hole corporate universities into School, College, or Academy types. The generic strategies constitute a framework that is meant as a guideline for strategic choices and better understanding of their consequences, and not as a normative template.

Exploratory research on the strategic profile of 21 different companies and governmental organizations has led to the hypothesis that most corporate universities pursue a predominantly School-type strategy and have the ambition to also develop College and Academy characteristics.[13] The general pattern that has emerged from the research and various strategy workshops with corporate university teams is that a large number of corporate universities combine School, College, and Academy characteristics while both the School type and to a lesser degree the College type dominate. The biggest two challenges seen by these corporate universities is the struggle with complexity, and a fuzzy organizational image that, in the worst case, boils down to "a sort of training department with a fancy name." In the management literature such challenges are associated with companies that suffer from a lack of strategic focus. In the words of Treacy and Wiersema (1995) they "play the average game" instead of focusing on a single generic strategy to excel.

Applied to corporate university strategy, this way of reasoning yields the picture given in Figure 3.3. The circle stands for a generally accepted level of corporate university performance, not markedly stronger or weaker than peers in the same industry or other benchmarks – quite in tune with playing the average game.[14] Time, resources and attention are spread over School, College, and some Academy activities. The different directions of the vectors in Figure 3.3 symbolize the different nature of these activities, described in greater detail in Table 3.1. Corporate universities with a wide spread of activities may continue doing this for many years, but also risk being overlooked or undervalued when management attention and budgets are allocated, which form the lifeblood of most corporate universities. A worst-case scenario in this respect arises if activities of the corporate university are not all up to standard as a result of inadequate focus, resulting further in the inadequacy of critical mass and attention.

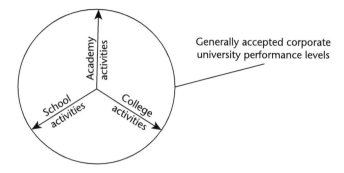

FIGURE 3.3 Playing the average game
Source: Analysis by the author

In situations like this, the corporate university leaders might need to revise their strategy following Figure 3.4 and, depending on the strategic needs of the organization served, to refocus the corporate strategy towards School, College, or Academy.

Corporate universities in large organizations may choose to disentangle their activities and split them into different units, as outlined in Figure 3.5, each focusing either on a School, College, or Academy type of strategy. Here, the underlying argument is to offer three distinct types of corporate university services while reaping the benefits of specialization and to reduce internal interaction costs (cf. Hagel and Singer, 1999).[15] It is prerequisite that the units have sufficient critical mass to excel without having to compete with one another for management attention. Mars University (described in Chapter 4) is an example, having established a unit called the Customized Learning Group. The unit serves as the innovation arm of the corporate university, dealing with business problems that cannot be anticipated by Mars University, and predominantly featuring Academy-type characteristics. Philips Lighting University (Chapter 10) follows a different approach, building the

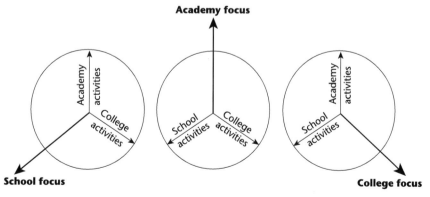

FIGURE 3.4 (Re)focused corporate university strategies
Source: Analysis by the author

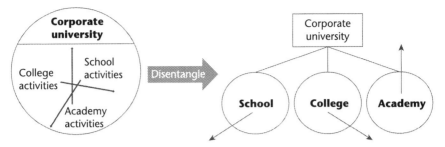

FIGURE 3.5 Disentangling the corporate university

Source: Analysis by the author

corporate university step by step. As a first step, large-scale, formal, and standardized learning solutions have been created and taken to a level of excellence to provide an answer to the challenge expressed in the motto "Bring speed to knowledge." After completion of this step and separation from the formal and standardized learning solutions, new approaches to informal learning for cross-border knowledge sharing and co-creation can be developed.

Conclusions

The strategy of a corporate university should fit with the strategy of the organization(s) served, like Russian matryoshka dolls.[16] Only then can the full learning potential of the organization be unlocked. For companies, this translates into competitive advantage; for institutions, it is a driving force strengthening the societal impact of the organization.

A loose fit between corporate university strategy and business strategy may lead to the proverbial "silver in the mine" as coined by Benjamin Franklin: fantastic potential in the organization remaining unused.[17] Few organizations can afford not to cultivate and reap the fruits of their learning capability in today's complex, dynamic, and demanding environment.

There are countless ways in which corporate university strategy can be aligned with the strategy of the organization. Three generic strategies can be discerned when combining the primal characteristics of organizational strategy and the strategic function of corporate universities:

- Corporate universities pursuing a School strategy primarily aim to sharpen and optimize current capabilities, helping their organizations to exploit the full potential of their current model. The value propositions, core activities, and resources of the corporate university form a tight system equipped to excel in *learning as usual* – revolving around effective knowledge transfer. Learning as usual may not sound very ambitious. However, successful *learning as usual* requires a high degree of professionalism, discipline, and expertise in the field of organizational learning.

- Corporate universities pursuing a College strategy primarily aim to drive organizational development and change, helping their organizations to implement a new business system. The value propositions, core activities, and resources of the corporate university form a tight and consistent system with which to excel in *transformational learning*, which is essential for organizations that place high importance in the actual act of adaptation, or, as Jeffrey Pfeffer and Robert Sutton (2000) call it, "Bridging the knowing-doing gap."
- Corporate universities pursuing an Academy strategy primarily aim to advance strategic renewal through innovation and new business development. The value propositions, core activities, and resources of the corporate university together form a system geared to excel in *exceptional learning*. This exploratory form of learning which crosses functions, business units, and organizational boundaries is essential in helping an organization adapt to changes in its environment, or to adapt an environment to its own advantage.

The School, College, and Academy strategies are helpful to broadly describe, discuss, and characterize corporate university business systems. Corporate universities can mirror themselves in these generic strategies and use them to analyze, envision, rethink, and reshape the way they create value for the organization. For some, it might mean accentuation and further development along the lines of a School strategy. For others, it would be setting out a new direction and moving towards a stronger focus on a strategy of the College or Academy type. Corporate universities trying to pursue the three distinctive strategies in a single organizational unit carry the risks of suboptimal results and a fuzzy image among organizational members. In such situations, disentangling, or refocusing the corporate university might be strategic options to explore. The strategic demands that corporate universities must fulfill to excel do not differ much from the demands that companies have to meet.

Notes

1 See Chapter 2 by Ron Meyer, which explains the concept of a business system. In essence, it deals with the system of crucial resources, activities, and propositions with which an organization creates value for a group of consumers (market).
2 Generic: not specific to a particular trade or organization.
3 Ambidexterity refers to the ability of people to use both right and left hands with equal ease. In the strategy literature the term is used to refer to organizations capable of simultaneously exploiting existing competencies and exploring new opportunities (Duncan, 1976; Kyriakopoulos and Moorman, 2004).
4 For example, the most profitable passenger jet in history is the Boeing 747, yielding billions of US$ for the company since its introduction in the 1970s. The design of the airplane stems from the 1960s. After numerous upgrades, the airplane is still in production, and the Boeing business system thriving on it has not changed very much over the past decades.
5 An example of "think different" preceding exploration is Apple Computers – the predecessor of Apple Inc. that, based on transformational thinking, started to move well beyond the computer manufacturer business system the company exploited up to the late 1990s (Lashinsky, 2012).

6 The term "Weberian" refers to the works of the twentieth-century German sociologist, philosopher, and political economist Max Weber, who is known as a principal architect of modern social science. The concept of ideal-type is described in his seminal work *Wirtschaft und Gesellschaft: Grundriss der Verstehender Soziologie* (Economy and Society: An Outline of Interpretive Sociology) published posthumously in 1922.
7 The practical aspect is the fact that managers and professionals who describe the current or desired characteristics of the business system describe how their organization is or should be attuned to its environment. In other words: the strategy of the organization.
8 Benelux: a geographical cluster of two autonomous countries (the Netherlands and Belgium) and a duchy (Luxembourg) in Western Europe.
9 De Alliantie, translated to English, is The Alliance. The name refers to the merger – and a subtle desire for autonomy – of three housing corporations that constituted the organization.
10 Many corporate universities in Continental Europe prefer to use the term "Academy" instead of "University." The term, however, does not refer to the corporate university strategy. Perhaps confusingly, the Alliantie Academie is a corporate university pursuing a College strategy.
11 In 2012 DHV merged with the smaller engineering, project management, and consulting company Royal Haskoning and became Royal HaskoningDHV with roots established in the UK, South Africa, and the Netherlands.
12 In the management literature such a setting is considered as a factor for innovation proficiency (McGrath, 2013).
13 The instrument used to capture the strategic profile of the corporate universities involved is called CU Profiler and comprises three general questions (e.g., when the corporate university was established), 12 questions to measure the preference for School, College or Academy characteristics, now and in the future, and one question about the strategy of the organization served, in terms of exploitation and exploration.
14 Figure 3.3 is a graphical representation of this reasoning, and builds on a basic figure from the works of Treacy and Wiersema (1995: 45).
15 The article about corporate strategy covers a relevant point but has also drawn criticism. Predictions made by the authors proved wrong. In the 1999 article, Yahoo! is praised as an industry leader, and the authors are skeptical about the survival of Amazon. Only a few years later, Yahoo! lost much ground to competitors (suffering from an inadequacy of strategic focus), while Amazon evolved into a leading web-retailer.
16 A matryoshka is a Russian wooden doll that contains further versions of itself nested in successively smaller dolls.
17 "Genius without education is like silver in the mine" (Benjamin Franklin, 1706–90, American scientist, inventor, statesman, and philosopher). See also Chapter 1 of this book.

Literature

Aronovitch, H. (2012). Interpreting Weber's Ideal-Types. *Philosophy of the Social Sciences*, Vol. 42, No. 3, pp. 356–69.
Duncan, R.B. (1976). The Ambidextrous Organization: Designing Dual Structures for Innovation. R.H. Kilmann, L.R. Pondy and D.P. Slevin (eds.) *The Management of Organization Design*, Vol. 1. *Strategies and Implementation*. North-Holland, New York, pp. 167–88.
McGrath, R.G. (2013). *The End of Competitive Advantage*. Boston: Harvard Business Review Press.
Hagel III, J. and M. Singer (1999), Unbundling the Corporation. *Harvard Business Review*, March–April, pp. 133–42.
Kim, C. and R. Mauborgne (2005). *Blue Ocean Strategy: How to Create Uncontested Market Space and Make the Competition Irrelevant*. Boston: Harvard Business School Press.
Knowles, M. (1984). *Andragogy in Action*. San Francisco: Jossey-Bass.

Kyriakopoulos, K. and C. Moorman (2004). Tradeoffs in Marketing Exploitation and Exploration Strategies: The Overlooked Role of Market Orientation. *International Journal of Research in Marketing*, Vol. 21, pp. 219–40.

Lafley, A.G., R.L. Martin, J.W. Rivkin, and N. Siggelkow (2012). Bringing Science to the Art of Strategy. *Harvard Business Review*, Sept., pp. 57–66.

Lashinsky, A. (2012). *Inside Apple: The Secrets Behind the Past and Future Success of Steve Job's Iconic Brand*. London: John Murray Publishers.

McGrath, R.G. (2013). *The End of Competitive Advantage*. Boston: Harvard Business Review Press.

Meyer, R. (2007). *Mapping the Mind of the Strategist: A Quantitative Methodology for Measuring the Strategic Beliefs of Executives*. Rotterdam: ERIM Ph.D. Series Research in Management 106.

Pfeffer, J. and R.I. Sutton (2000). *The Knowing-Doing Gap: How Smart Companies Turn Knowledge into Action*. Boston: Harvard Business School Press.

Porter, M. (1980). *Competitive Strategy: Techniques for Analyzing Industries and Competitors*. New York: The Free Press.

— (1985). *Competitive Advantage: Creating and Sustaining Superior Performance*. New York: The Free Press.

Rademakers, M. (2001). Hoe Strategisch is Uw Corporate University? Drie Generieke Niveaus van Corporate University Ontwikkeling. *Opleiding & Ontwikkeling*, Vol. 14, No. 4, pp. 15–18.

— (2005). Corporate Universities: Driving Force of Knowledge Innovation. *Journal of Workplace Learning*, Vol. 17, No. 1/2, pp. 130–36.

— (2012). *Corporate Universities: Aanjagers van de Lerende Organisatie*. Deventer: Kluwer.

Raisch, S., J. Birkinshaw, G. Probst, and M.L. Tushman (2009). Organizational Ambidexterity: Balancing Exploitation and Exploration for Sustained Performance. *Organization Science*, Vol. 20, No. 4, pp. 685–95.

Roth, G. and C. Wittich (eds.) (1978). *Max Weber: Economy and Society*. Berkeley: University of California Press.

Senge, P. (1990). *The Fifth Discipline: The Art & Practice of the Learning Organization*. New York: Currency Doubleday.

Treacy, M. and F. Wiersema (1995). *The Discipline of Market Leaders*. New York: Basic Books.

4
CORPORATE UNIVERSITY VALUE CREATION AND LEARNING FORMATS

Co-authors: Ron Meyer and Han van der Pool

> We can't solve problems by using the same kind
> of thinking we used when we created them.
> –*Albert Einstein*

This chapter revolves around the questions of how corporate universities create value for their organizations and which learning formats they deploy. Two instruments are introduced to explore these two questions in more detail: the Value Creation Menu and the Learning Formats Model. They will be discussed and illustrated with examples from corporate universities across a wide range of industries, companies, and countries. Some of the examples of value creation by corporate universities that will be presented are Kenya Airways (East Africa), Pertamina (Indonesia), VolkerWessels, IHC Merwede, RWS (the Netherlands), CRH (Ireland), Haniel (Germany), Deloitte, Mars, Disney, and Apple (US), operating in the airline, energy, construction, shipbuilding, water management, infrastructure, trading, professional services, confectionery, entertainment, and high-tech industries.

The Value Creation Menu and Learning Formats Model will be combined and applied to three internationally operating corporate universities: Ahold (leading retailer in Europe and US), Heineken (global leader in the premium beer market), and TNT (worldwide postal and parcel services).[1] At the end of this chapter, Pixar University will be exemplified as a source of inspiration for corporate universities rethinking how they want to create value and which learning formats to use in the future.

Corporate university value creation

Whether choosing to be a school, college or academy,[2] corporate universities need to understand clearly how they want to create value. They need to have a sense of

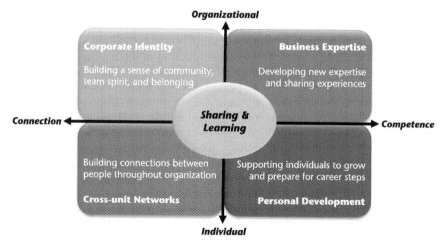

FIGURE 4.1 Corporate university Value Creation Menu
Source: Meyer, 2012

the intended impact on their organizations. Do they want to create value by building competences or by building relationships? Or both? And do they want to focus on creating value at the individual level or at the collective level? Or both? When these two dimensions of value creation (competence development vs. connecting people, and organizational vs. individual development) are combined into a value creation "menu card," a matrix is formed (Figure 4.1) with four distinctive corporate university value-creation options: personal development, cross-unit networks, corporate identity, and business expertise. They are described in more detail below.

- Personal development option: individual learning, competence driven
  This option is most common among corporate universities at present. It is close to the traditional role of learning and development departments in companies – and it is often the unit from which corporate universities evolve. In essence, the personal development option means that the corporate university helps (future) employees to achieve higher competence levels – for the benefit of the organization. The learning activities are often linked with career paths, talent development, and succession plans, and also with strategy, in the sense that the organization has access to sufficient numbers of people with the right competences to fulfill plans made.

  Corporate universities like the Pride Center of Kenya Airlines (est. 2010), the corporate university of the Indonesian state oil company Pertamina (est. 2012), and the company school of the Dutch shipbuilder IHC Merwede (on the brink of being closed down in 2008, but thriving in 2013) are primarily driven by the personal development option. Avoiding or overcoming shortages of employees with the right qualifications forms an important and clear rationale behind their fundamental choices.

For instance, the Pride Center helps Kenya Airlines (and other airlines in Eastern Africa) to secure access to sufficient numbers of competent cabin and ground handling crew, cargo handlers, and accident investigators, to name a few functions.[3] The Pertamina corporate university evolved from the learning and development unit of the company in 2012, organizing competency-based training and a number of pilot projects in the field of engineering, sales, and maintenance. Now, in 2013, the corporate university offers what it calls competency-driven education at the individual level: companywide, linked to business needs, cost efficient, and based on personal road maps.[4] IHC Merwede company-specific education is offered to technicians ranging from metal workers to engineers, enabling the organization to stay abreast of the competition in the high-end market for seagoing vessels with special functions and properties.[5]

The value-creation option of personal development can also be seen as the starting point for establishing the Shell Project Academy (as the company foresaw dramatic shortages of qualified project managers), but also the Shell Commercial Academy.[6] More options were added as the corporate universities progressed over time. Pertamina corporate university is taking the same path, aiming for current and future business-issue-driven organizational learning.[7] It is well in accordance with the general observation that the potential of corporate universities is much larger than competence development at the individual level.

- Cross-unit network option: individual learning, connection driven
  Although individual learning is key, competence development is not what this option is about. Corporate universities with a focus on this option often do not even carry the name of "academy" or "university." Rather, these are units, small teams or even individual executives who connect individuals with the aim to promote cross-department, cross-business unit, cross-discipline, and cross-border cooperation for the benefit of the organization. Achieving synergies can be seen as a strategic rationale behind this corporate university option. The corporate university, in any type or shape, offers platforms where people inside and sometimes also outside the organization can come to know each other through working together outside their daily jobs. Topics on which they work together tend to be business issue driven, requiring people to connect in order to cope with challenges they meet along the way – or bring with them.

  Examples of individual connection-driven corporate universities are the corporate academy of the Ireland-based corporation CRH (an internationally leading company in the field of building materials), DHV University (of the global engineering company DHV, operating in 35 countries around the world[8]), VolkerWessels Academy (described below), Haniel Academy (of the German family-owned conglomerate Haniel[9]), and the community of project managers that form the cornerstone of the Shell Project Academy.

It is not hard to identify the rationale behind the focus which CRH, DHV and VolkerWessels place on connecting people: A large number of business units across different areas of expertise and geographies need to be linked, while maintaining a high level of autonomy and market responsiveness. However, the primary focus of connecting people is not always easily discerned in the programs, which are commonly labeled as management development programs or shaped as conferences revolving around a strategic issue. For instance, DHV University is known for its extensive program enabling business managers to connect and share their ideas in order to further business development.[10] In a similar fashion, CRH runs conferences which gather senior managers from units across the company and help them shape their visions around future opportunities and challenges. Programs can also be ongoing in nature, as in the Shell Project Academy and the VolkerWessels Academy, which are both deeply rooted in the value-creation options of individual learning, connection driven. For other corporate universities, such as Haniel Academy, connecting people is a "collateral benefit" of corporate training activities aimed at individual competence development, rather than the focus. This seems true for many corporate universities around the world, which means they have much unused potential to reap for their organizations.

- Business expertise option: organizational learning, competence driven
  Corporate universities can also have their center of gravity in the area of developing new business expertise and sharing knowledge across the organization. An example is the Customised Learning Group (CLG) that serves as the innovation arm of Mars University, the corporate university of the American food and confectionery company Mars (described in Chapter 5). Among other objectives, CLG looks for trends and delivers interventions to help Mars units address new business challenges and issues. In addition, one of the programs of the broader Mars University combines organizational learning with competence development. The program focuses on key debates, tensions, and strategic choices facing the Mars Corporation in the future in the fields of, among others, sustainability and business strategy.

  Another example is Deloitte University (of the global professional services company Deloitte Touche Tohmatsu, headquartered in the US) for which the business expertise option is pivotal. It is directly linked with the Deloitte strategic priorities of building deep industry knowledge and being an innovation catalyst (described in Chapter 6).

  An example in the area of governmental organizations is the Corporate Learning Center of RWS[11] (the main executive body of the Dutch Ministry of Infrastructure and Environment). To help RWS gain access to new expertise the Corporate Learning Center collaborates on a structural basis with companies and institutions. Together with these organizations new learning and development programs are created to renew joint processes, techniques, and practices.

- Corporate identity option: organizational learning, connection driven

  For many companies, protecting, reproducing, and transferring the corporate culture is a top strategic priority. The rationale is that a unique corporate culture enables value creation in a unique way that is very hard – if possible at all – to copy by the competition. Their corporate university programs revolve around establishing a strong sense of community, with team spirit, a common language, and belonging, driven by shared corporate values.

  Companies widely known for their corporate universities pursuing the corporate identity option include Apple, Mars, and Disney.[12] Apple University was established in 2011 in Cupertino, California, not long before the founder and CEO of the company, Steve Jobs, passed away (Lashinsky, 2012). It has been placed in a position to retain the unique Apple culture of innovation, following the credo of "Think Different" (Lashinsky, 2011). The corporate university is seen as an important contributor to the future success of the company. The same is true for the large and broad Mars corporate that disseminates the Mars Five Principles constituting the corporate identity. As demanded by Mars top management, all programs featured by the corporate university have the five Mars principles and culture embedded.

  Disney University has a focus on individual development, based on transferring highly standardized and codified knowledge, but also that of a highly codified corporate identity. The high standards of perfection can be seen as a component of this identity. All people starting to work for Disney are obliged to follow the Disney Traditions Program during their first day on the job. In this program, the Disney policy, code of conduct, and rules of the game are passed on. The program is offered in training centers located close to all major locations of the company around the world. All efforts are, in the end of the day, aimed at securing the carefully codified services of the company and the general value proposition known as the "Disney experience."

It is safe to say that the more value-creation options a corporate university pursues, the higher the corporate university organizational complexity becomes. For instance, Shell Project Academy (described in Chapter 7) covers all areas except building corporate identity, and it is among the largest and most complex corporate universities in the world.

Whatever the value-creation options a corporate university focuses on, they can be used as a point of reference when shaping and executing the corporate university strategy.[13] More in particular, they help to make clear what key stakeholders can expect from the corporate university – and what not. VolkerWessels, for example, is an international construction company composed of no less than 125 highly autonomous business units scattered across sectors and countries such as the UK, Canada, and the Netherlands. Their VolkerWessels Academy is very clear about what it does, and what it does not do. Its focus is on "connecting individual managers across the organization" through learning programs. In the words of the CFO of the company:

> The Academy is the place where VolkerWessels gets together.

If requests from the business units to provide courses and programs are not in tune with the VolkerWessels Academy focus on being a "connector," they are turned down.[14]

Corporate university learning formats

Great variety can be found in the learning formats deployed by corporate universities, i.e., the approaches to learning that they use to shape knowledge transfer, sharing and creation within and between organizations. Figure 4.2 provides a model featuring an inventory of the most important learning formats seen at corporate universities. The model is a three-layered taxonomy integrating a layer of learning styles (e.g., reflecting, planning), a second layer with ways to promote learning (e.g., gaming, investigating), and as a third layer the way these learning activities are packaged (e.g., in a course or a case). Put together, they form four distinctive learning formats. Corporate universities can be compared and contrasted on the basis of these formats, and individual organizations can

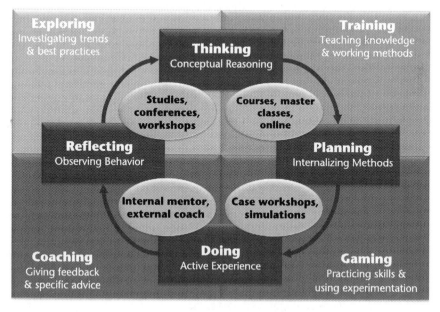

FIGURE 4.2 Corporate university Learning Formats Model

Source: Meyer, 2012

reflect on the balance between the value-creation options they pursue and the formats used with regard to corporate learning.

The underlying logic of the Learning Formats Model is structured along the lines of the widely known learning cycle concept conceived by David Kolb (1984). The learning cycle offers a common point of reference, depicting learning by trial and error (Doing), observation (Reflecting), conceptual reasoning (Thinking), and testing what was learned (Planning) in relation to each other. The cycle can be started at any point, but learning through experience is usually taken as the point of departure.

To explore different kinds of corporate university learning formats, a useful starting point is the Thinking step: What are we going to do? More in particular: What do we think that people in the organization need to learn? Which working methods and techniques should be deployed? Next, the arrow from Thinking to Planning stands for the act of moving through the learning format known as Training. It stands for activities corporate universities organize, such as courses, master classes, and e-learning – all aimed at enabling people in the organization to acquire knowledge that is new to them as individuals.

The next arrow in the model, from Planning to Doing, involves the learning format of Gaming. It is about practicing the learned material in a delimited setting, through activities like cases, workshops, and simulation. This learning format is important, making sure that what is learned in theory actually sticks in the mind. If people who are sent to a course only gain new knowledge and return to their jobs the same as before, there is likely to be a low return on investment in the course program.

Next, the step of Doing occurs where people do their jobs – using what they have learned, but also meeting new challenges as unexpected things happen and problems emerge. When learning by trial and error to find answers to newly emerging questions falls short, the next learning format comes into play: Coaching, symbolized in the model by the arrow from Doing to Reflecting. Feedback and situation-specific advice help people in their jobs understand why things do not work as expected. Reflection – to achieve acceptance and understanding that old solutions and routines do not tend to work in the face of new problems – forms the stepping stone towards the last step in the learning cycle: It is the move from Reflecting to Thinking through the learning format of Exploring.

The Exploring learning format is about the act of looking for new solutions to newly emerged problems that might either be unique (requiring investigation) or are similar to questions already solved by other organizations (best practices). The outcomes feed the stage of Thinking again: What else should we do? Missing pieces of knowledge required to see things differently enter the learning format of Training, starting a new cycle of learning.

The Value Creation Menu and Learning Formats Model can be used in combination with each other for comparative research on corporate universities at organizational, industry, national, and cross-national levels of analysis. More practically, the models also help corporate universities to systematically review themselves for the purpose of their strategy development, and to compare their value-creation focus and learning formats with peers for inspiration.

Combining the Value Creation Menu and Learning Formats Model helps to investigate which learning formats the corporate university needs to adopt or develop further to meet the value-creation option(s) it has chosen to pursue. The questions that can be derived from this are: Which value-creation options do we pursue at present? Which one(s) should we pursue in the light of the latent and/or manifest needs of the organization(s) we serve? Next, what is the portfolio of learning formats deployed by the corporate university? What are present or emerging gaps in our portfolio?

Corporate university value creation and learning formats in practice

Heineken and Ahold are multinationals that established their corporate universities more than a decade ago. The Heineken University and the Ahold Retail Academy have existed since 1998. TNT (with roots dating back to 1799) has a long history of learning and development, but not under the banner of an "academy" or "university." Over time, the corporate universities of Heineken, Ahold, and TNT have been served by the same dean, Han van der Pool, which makes it possible to describe their value-creation focus and learning formats from an insider's perspective. Exhibit 4.1 provides a condensed profile of the companies involved.

The corporate universities are described below, comparing and contrasting them with each other to shed more light on questions such as the following. Which of the

---

EXHIBIT 4.1: COMPANY PROFILES OF HEINEKEN, AHOLD, AND TNT

Heineken employs over 60,000 people and is active in more than 170 countries, with a focus on producing, distributing, and selling premium beer.[15] It is a publicly listed company, with the Heineken family descendants holding a controlling share.

Ahold is a publicly listed retailing company with firm roots in grocery in the US (with formulas such as Stop & Shop, Giant Food, and Peapod) and Europe (Albert Heijn). In 2012, the company operated over 3,000 stores and employed more than 225,000 people worldwide.[16]

TNT is the fourth-largest express and parcel services in the world, employing 75,000 people worldwide. This publicly listed company can be seen as the product of a former state-owned firm in the area of postal services that went public and grew into an international company through acquisitions (such as the takeover of the Australian express firm TNT in 1996).[17]

learning formats (shown in Figure 4.2) did the corporate universities adopt or develop to support the value-creation options they chose (depicted in Figure 4.1)? What are the most important differences and commonalities between the corporate universities? What conclusions can we draw from this analysis?

All three corporate universities have been established with an emphasis on the value-creation option of personal development. The importance of this option is exemplified most clearly by the Heineken University Manifesto, which functions as a directive for all Heineken University programs:

> Enjoyment is essential to learning. Learning is essential for personal development. Personal development leads to personal success. Personal success is behind company success. Learn to change – Change to learn.[18]

Taking a closer view of what the Heineken University actually does when serving about 1,500 internal clients on an annual basis, it appears that the corporate university has begun to create value on a broader basis than the apparent predominance of personal development. An important focus of the corporate university is to drive organizational learning through connecting Heineken managers and employees from all over the world. Examples are the (learning) Communities of Practice (CoP) set up and facilitated by Heineken University. CoPs are self-managed communities including 50 to 5,000 functional managers and employees who are geared by the corporate university to exchange best practices, and, in some instances, to build new expertise. Some CoPs gather physically, while others make use of web-based instruments such as web conferencing and instant messaging. For instance, HRD managers avoid reinventing the wheel by sharing their communication training courses; marketing managers share their insights in making the Heineken brand more fashionable among younger generations of beer drinkers, and more in general, community members get each other in touch with external experts, certified knowledge, and relevant literature.

The Heineken University was established at the instigation of top management, who saw importance for the company in taking better advantage of knowledge. Initially taking a personal development focus to secure competence development in the area of building and understanding brands – which is the lifeblood of the company – learning formats of the training type have been developed. E-learning has become an important way to provide personalized training. Next, much in tune with top management demand, the corporate university has branched out towards community building to drive learning through knowledge exchange. The number of learning formats has been broadened accordingly. Training formats have been enriched with working methods for cross-border functional teams, and (peer to peer) coaching and conference-based approaches have been added to the corporate university repertoire to facilitate and enable effective community-based learning.

The Ahold Retail Academy stresses corporate talent development, which is all about personal development when it comes to learning in the organization.

The Retail Academy does not cover practical skills training, as this is addressed on a local level by business units across the US and Europe. The corporate university was established in 1998 and was quick to launch a flagship program aimed at the development of management talents in the company. In close cooperation with Cornell University (US), the Retail Academy developed a customized management development program. This corporate university also took the role of linking pin between headquarters ("the holding") and local and regional management to ensure alignment of expectations and needs. Managers identified as top talent by the company are invited to join the Retail Academy program. In terms of impact, it is safe to say that almost all top positions within Ahold are now held by the graduates of the program.

Training and simulation are the dominant training formats used by the Retail Academy. Combinations of lectures by Ahold managers, functional specialists, and external marketing and retail professors ensure knowledge transfer. A supermarket management simulation, featured as a business game, covers practical issues revolving around strategic choices and various supermarket formats. A desirable side effect of the way the learning formats are shaped – for example, bringing the participants together multiple times in group settings – is the creation of long lasting cross-unit networks throughout the company.

Just like Ahold Retail Academy, talent development also dominates the learning and development activities at TNT. Personal development is central to the corporate university activities and also explicitly linked with the TNT strategy. For instance, corporate social responsibility plays an important role in the strategy of the company, and hence is reflected in leadership development (Van der Pool, 2010). Leadership at TNT is perceived as a mindset embedded in everyday behavior. Hence, when the TNT predecessor TPG was split into PostNL and TNT, corporate social responsibility continued to be reflected in the strategies and leadership behavior of both newly formed companies.

TNT perceives talent development as a mission critical corporate process. For good reasons. Being the worldwide No. 4, and competing for talent with much larger organizations like FedEx and UPS, makes the capability to gain access to the best people in the parcel and express industry a strategic advantage. Filling the organization-wide management talent pipeline and keeping it filled is viewed as an absolute necessity. The process of management development is also included in the TNT business cycle, making it a recurring process instead of a set of one-time initiatives, and linking strategy formation with leadership development.

Research on learning interventions required to execute new strategies at TNT are a corporate university responsibility. The research efforts are aimed at finding answers to the questions discussed above:[19] What do we think that people in the organization need to learn? Which working methods and techniques should be deployed? The TNT top management team needs the answers, as they carry the responsibility for talent development. Moreover, the top management team members, including the CEO, are directly involved in the set of learning formats used for leadership development. They are active as coaches, mentors, and trainers in order to share their experiences and insights. Strategy and learning are connected in this approach, as high potentials are linked to experienced leaders and explore and study critical corporate issues.

Comparing and contrasting the corporate universities of Heineken, Ahold, and TNT, it is not difficult to see the importance of the traditional option of value creation through personal development. Another commonality is that the corporate universities use personal development as a stepping stone towards the realization of a broader set of value-creation options, including community building and, to some degree, new business expertise development. The move towards a broader scope has been a deliberate part of the corporate university strategy at Heineken. By contrast, at Ahold and TNT the broader scope can rather be perceived as attractive side effects of the learning formats primarily aimed for personal development purposes. These side effects may well be an important lever for corporate university development, if their value and unrealized potential for the company are recognized by senior management. Learning formats usually follow the corporate university value-creation focus, but the scope of value creation may also follow unintended side effects of learning formats.

Corporate universities of the future

At present a majority of corporate universities seems to focus on value creation through personal development. Nonetheless, the pressure on corporate universities to shift part of their value-creating activities towards organizational development is rising.[20] This is not because it is the latest fashion, but because the purpose of corporate universities is to make sure that their organizations take as much advantage of learning as possible – as is exemplified by Heineken University.

Corporate universities are also likely to put a stronger emphasis on building connections between people throughout the organization, and to support a collective team spirit and belonging. Personal development is more and more a hygiene factor, while distinctive advantages for organizations are to be found in the realm of people sharing and building knowledge together, and making a difference as a collective with a cause. If this holds true, the value-creation options of building cross-unit networks and corporate identity (Figure 4.2) will gain importance. An iconic company like Pixar, based in California, US, can be seen as an inspiring example. The company puts strong emphasis on teamwork, serving internal clients with fun and spontaneity, while not forgoing discipline and hard work. Pixar sees as its long-term goal to:

> Combine proprietary technology and world-class creative talent to develop computer-animated feature films with memorable characters and heartwarming stories that appeal to all ages.[21]

This long-term goal or vision forms the imperative to build a creative climate, and also to forge a strong *esprit de corps* centered on mutual respect and trust. In tune, failure is celebrated just as much as successes. Play is a key feature of the company culture, as is reflected in the offices and studios of the company, which are designed like a corporate playground. The Pixar University activities are aimed to support this culture. Rather than being the focus of value creation, personal development is a positive by-product of pursuing a strong Pixar corporate identity and cross-Pixar networks as well as building new business-relevant expertise. In terms of learning formats, teaching happens through storytelling and storyboarding to display ideas. Moreover, knowledge sharing through internal and external collaboration is encouraged. "Doing" happens in accordance with the credo of "Fun, play, and celebrations." Learning through reflection and thinking are embedded in "postmortems" (sessions aimed at learning from successes and mistakes).

In tune with the Pixar leadership, more and more leaders subscribe to the idea of seizing the value of learning to fulfill strategic aims – even in times of deep economic crisis. Deliberate use of organizational learning to optimize, implement, and renew strategy is reflected in five common trends in value creation by corporate universities:

- more programs to further organization-specific knowledge sharing (i.e., cross-unit networks and business expertise),
- more leadership development directly linked to strategy (i.e., personal development and business expertise),
- more custom-made programs in which strategic issues are handled (i.e., corporate identity and business expertise),
- more personal development paths, with personal coaching and assignments (i.e., personal development),
- a stronger connection between corporate university programs and talent management (i.e., personal development).

In addition, learning formats are influenced and change as the result of computer and internet-driven innovations. Both the ways and sources of learning available to organizations and individuals have widened and the end of this development is not in sight. Gaming and simulation are still in their infancy and expected to gain territory as learning formats of choice. Deemed old fashioned in the light of the rapid proliferation of e-learning based learning formats, though, classroom learning (or better: *high touch learning*)[22] has been rediscovered as an important way to establish and maintain communities for knowledge sharing, creating new business expertise and building a joint corporate identity.

Concluding remarks

Corporate universities need to make sure that learning hits organization needs. Hence, they constantly need to review their options for value creation and renew their learning formats. Should corporate universities just stick to the traditional activities aimed at personal development, or also cover the fields of corporate identity, cross-unit networks, or business expertise? Should the range of learning formats be extended, adding (more) gaming, coaching, and exploration to corporate university programs?

Personal development is likely to remain an important activity for many corporate universities – and a stepping stone towards a broader role in the organization. As a rule, however, the more value-creation options and learning formats that are pursued, the more complex a corporate university gets. It will not be easy to strike a balance between strategic focus on the one hand, and avoiding a tunnel vision on the other. Organizational pressures to broaden and to expand the scope of value-creation options covered and learning formats offered reflect the rise of a more complex, dynamic, and hyper-connected world. The challenge for corporate universities will be to stay aligned from the outside-in, i.e., opportunity-driven, but also from the inside-out to build on current strengths and avoid throwing the baby out with the bathwater.[23]

Corporate universities are not short of instruments, models, and inspiring examples when rethinking their options for value creation and learning formats. Rethinking, however, is just a first step. New and impactful arrangements need to be dreamt up, tested, implemented, practiced, and assessed as the input for the next cycle of learning. Leading corporate universities of the future are likely to practice what they preach.

Notes

1 The three corporate universities are addressed by Han van der Pool, with his analysis benefiting from first-hand knowledge of the organizations involved.
2 See Chapter 3 of this book for an explanation of these corporate university strategy types.
3 Source: Kenya Airlines company information.
4 Source: Research by the authors, Pertamina company documents, discussions with Pertamina officials, and observers.
5 Source: Desk research by the authors.
6 The Shell Commercial Academy started in 2005 with the objective to train staff to better negotiate with organizations in control of oil and gas resources – often governments.
7 Source: Corporate university overview from www.scribd.com/doc/125582169/Pertamina-Corporate-University-Overview.
8 In 2012, DHV merged with the smaller engineering, project management and consulting company Royal Haskoning, and became Royal HaskoningDHV with roots established in the UK, South Africa, and the Netherlands.
9 Haniel, headquartered in Duisburg, Germany, is active in industries ranging from washroom hygiene to pharmaceuticals and business equipment to stainless steel trade.
10 Source: Rademakers (2012).
11 RWS stands for *Rijkswaterstaat*. It is the Dutch governmental organization responsible for efficient and safe transportation on the national roads and waterways. The organization also ensures that the country – being largely situated below sea level – is defended against floods and has access to safe and clean water.
12 Shaping a uniform corporate identity is also top priority of many companies much smaller than these three USA-based global giants. An example is the Boarding Program for new recruits at Exademy, the corporate university of software company Exact.

13 Chapter 3 covers the topic of corporate university strategy.
14 Source: Rademakers (2012).
15 Apart from the global Heineken brand, the company exploits a portfolio of regional and national brands including Moretti, Zywiec, Star, Bintang, Primus, and Tiger Beer.
16 Source: Company document Ahold at a Glance, 2012.
17 Through the years, the name of the company has changed from PTT, KPN, TPG to TNT. More recently, in 2011, the postal services on the one hand, and express and parcel services on the other, were split into PostNL and TNT Express.
18 Source: Van der Pool (2005).
19 These questions are part of the Learning Format Model (Figure 4.1).
20 This conclusion is drawn from observations in the field, and also from the outcomes of a self assessment instrument called the Corporate University Profiler. A vast majority of users of this web-based instrument indicate the operation as a corporate university focusing on personal development, and with the ambition to add organizational-level learning services.
21 Source: Capodagli and Jackson (2009).
22 The concept of *high touch learning* stands for all methods aiming to deepen and intensify contact among the participants in a program (Van der Pool, 2004). High touch learning revolves around openness and exploration, driven by mutual connections. An example of high touch learning is a corporate university program involving different people, to explore new ways for in-company coaching. High touch learning seems at odds with *high tech learning* (e-learning). More of the one will lead to the demise of the other. In practice, however, the tension between high touch and high tech can be seen as a paradox open to creative combinations of both (seemingly) opposite approaches to learning in organizations.
23 The term outside-in refers to a strategic perspective (Porter, 1980). It stands for the idea that organizations must identify new opportunities in their environment, and then adapt their business system to stay fit. The opposite, inside-out strategy (Miller et al., 2002), however, is equally important. It stands for the idea that organizations must identify the strategic resources that are part of their business system, and use and rearrange them to move successfully into existing markets – or create new ones. For organizations to reap their full strategic potential, they need to make fruitful combinations of outside-in and inside-out strategies (Meyer, 2007). The difficulty is that genuine inside-out and outside-in strategies tend to be opposites.

Literature

Burchell, M. and J. Robin (2011). *The Great Workplace: How to Build It, How to Keep it and Why it Matters*. San Francisco: Jossey-Bass.

Capodagli, B. and L. Jackson (2009). *Innovation the Pixar Way*. New York: McGraw-Hill

Kolb, D.A. (1984). *Experiential Learning: Experience as the Source of Learning and Development*. Englewood Cliffs, NJ: Prentice-Hall.

Lashinsky, A. (2011). *Fortune Magazine*, No. 7, June.

— (2012). *Inside Apple: How America's Most Admired and Secretive Company Really Works*. London: John Murray Publishers.

Meister, J.C. and K. Willyerd (2010). *The 2020 Workplace: How Innovative Companies Attract, Develop, and Keep Tomorrow's Employees Today*. New York: HarperBusiness.

Meyer, R. (2007). *Mapping the Mind of the Strategist: A Quantitative Methodology for Measuring the Strategic Beliefs of Executives*. Rotterdam: ERIM Ph.D. Series Research in Management 106.

— (2012). *Learning to Learn: Unleashing the Potential of Your Corporate University. Conference presentation*. Corporate University Event, Erasmus University Rotterdam.

Miller, D., R. Eisenstat and N. Foote (2002). Strategy from the Inside-out: Building Capability-creating Organizations. *California Management Review*. Vol. 33, No. 3.

Pool, H. van der (2004). Trends in Leadership Development. *Tijdschrift voor Management Development*, Vol. 12, No. 1.

Pool, H. van der (2005), Lerende netwerken organiseren in een virtuele omgeving. In: G.J. Schuiling and W. Heine (eds.) *Leren stimuleren*. Assen: Van Gorkum.

Pool, H. van der and J. Töller (2008). Een Helder Profiel van HRD. *Leren in Organisaties*. Vol. 8, No. 11.

Pool, H. van der (2010). Top Companies for Leaders. *Tijdschrift voor Management Development*, Vol. 18, No. 2.

Porter, M.E. (1980). *Competitive Strategy: Techniques for Analyzing Competitors and Industries*. New York: The Free Press.

Rademakers, M.F.L. (2012). *Corporate Universities: Aanjagers van de Lerende Organisatie*. Deventer: Kluwer.

5

MARS UNIVERSITY: RAISING THE BAR

Co-author: Paul Hunter

> Through learning we re-create ourselves.
> −Peter M. Senge

Mars, Inc. is the third largest privately owned company in the US. If it were on the Fortune 500 list, it would be in the top 100, ahead of McDonald's, Starbucks, and General Mills. At McLean, Virginia, however, the Mars Corporate Office impresses with a tone of austerity, much unlike the large, luxurious tower where one might expect to find the headquarters of a multibillion dollar corporation. Along with global brands that include M&M's, Snickers, Wrigley, Uncle Ben's, and Whiskas, the company has earned a reputation for excellence in corporate learning, which has evolved over the years. Its top management clearly relies on the Mars corporate university to keep the company aligned with an increasingly dynamic business environment.

Important developments in the business world that are of significance to Mars include an increasing depletion in the quality and quantity of non-renewable natural resources and the need to establish greater balance between business and societal interests. The most important of those predominant conflicts is the effect of economic stagnation in Western economies weighed against opportunity generated in rapidly emerging economies in other parts of the world, in particular Asia. The key strategic challenge for Mars is best described in the words of its president, Paul S. Michaels,[1] who sees Mars' contribution to "the resolution of not only an industry challenge, but a challenge that faces all of humankind" in the following questions:

> How shall we preserve the environment for future generations, how can we spread prosperity and economic growth more universally, and how will we feed more than seven billion people while also addressing the challenge of obesity?

The way Mars anticipates and responds to changes in the business environment is strongly influenced by its core values, enunciated through a set of five guiding principles: Quality, Responsibility, Mutuality, Efficiency, and Freedom. Strategy at Mars is grounded in the entrenched culture formed with a core objective first expressed by its founding father, Forrest E. Mars, Sr. as the creation of "a mutuality of benefits for all stakeholders."[2]

The Five Principles of Mars are again the fundamental components of a strategic change agenda that was initiated halfway through the first decade of the new millennium and revised toward the end of the decade. Starting with a somewhat evolutionary approach to change, its primary objective was the realization of efficiency and effectiveness on a company-wide basis. Results were realized mostly in the form of cost reductions and restructuring.

The momentum for change has increased dramatically in recent years and is now far more revolutionary in nature. At the same time, the degree of complexity associated with the strategic issues it faces has meant that resolution is far more difficult and demanding than before. Appropriate outcomes are essential though, as the company's long-term sustainability and growth rely on getting it right. The revised strategic change agenda is an integral driver of Mars' global growth ambition – one that is far more attuned to the changing demands not only of its customers, but the global consumers of its products and services as well.

Education has always played an important role in the company, in times of both gradual and rapid change. This chapter discusses the strategic role of Mars University in helping the company to transform and reshape its business over the years. We show how the corporate university has moved from an internationally decentralized ad hoc training operation to a globally unified driver of learning that fulfills the role of a key enabler of strategy.

Origin and nature of the company

Mars' origins date back to 1911, when Frank C. Mars commenced business as a manufacturer and distributor of chocolate-based confectionery in the US. Today, the company employs more than 72,000 *associates*[3] in its global operations. These are located in 74 countries; its facilities consist of 134 manufacturing or R&D sites and 360 offices. To get to the size that it has, Mars has grown through organic and inorganic means. The Wrigley segment (chewing gum and confectionery) for example, was the result of a US$22 billion acquisition that was completed in 2008. Mars' annual global revenue now exceeds US$33 billion, but even with this size and reach it has only three shareholders, each of them a grandchild of the founder, Frank C. Mars: Forrest E. Mars, Jr., John Franklyn Mars, and Jacqueline Badger.

The Mars company structure is aligned around core/primary functions (such as Finance, People and Organization, Research and Development) and six business segments (Chocolate, Petcare, Wrigley, Food, Drinks, Symbioscience). Each segment is responsible for the management of some of the company's global brands.

The Five Mars Principles

Quality	Responsibility	Mutuality	Efficiency	Freedom
• The consumer is our boss, quality is our work and value for money is our goal.	• As individuals, we demand total responsibility from ourselves; as associates, we support the responsibilities of others.	• A mutual benefit is a shared benefit; a shared benefit will endure.	• We use resources to the full, waste nothing and do only what we can do best.	• We need freedom to shape our future; we need profit to remain free.

FIGURE 5.1 The Five Mars Principles

Source: Adapted from the Mars corporate website

The Five Principles of Mars (illustrated in Figure 5.1) are taken very seriously by the company. Their imagery is displayed on the walls of every Mars office in the world. They embed the culture, motivate and engage associates, guide strategic decision making, and strengthen the relationship between the company and the stakeholders with whom it interacts. Mars corporate strategy is communicated through the metaphor "Our Principles in Action." The new generation of Mars family members who work in the business today consider the Five Principles to be the cornerstone of the company:

> We at Mars share special values about our company and the way it should be run. These values – our Five Principles – set us apart from others, requiring that we think and act differently towards our associates, our brands and our business. These principles have always been demanding and are an essential part of our heritage. We believe they are the real reason for our success. They keep us true to ourselves at times of growth and guide us reliably when we are challenged.

The description of the Responsibility principle in Figure 5.1 refers to the people who work for Mars as associates. Forrest E. Mars, Sr. always saw their contributions as more than just being a person on the payroll. He preferred instead to support individual pursuit of ambition and personal development as leaders in a way that would allow them to make a difference in their local communities and elsewhere. This approach gives Mars associates every reason to develop a long, rewarding career with the company.

Mars University *avant la lettre*

In the years that are representative of Mars' birth, adolescence, and international growth, there was no physical or formal construction in the form of a corporate university. There was, though, a strong commitment to employee development.

During the years from the 1920s through to the late 1990s Mars was known to have given substantial support to the training and development of a large number of skilled and unskilled workers. Initially, this included thousands of people who provided manual labor in the areas of manufacturing and distribution as well as other support environments. During the first phase of the development of Mars education programs most forms of learning were provided through on-the-job training. These were supported in later years with specialist training programs that were conducted internally or outside the company.

All education programs at Mars evolved in a wide range of styles and formats, from the time that Mars grew out of its original factory to become a significant company on a global scale. An example is the format that emerged in China (see Exhibit 5.1).

EXHIBIT 5.1: EMERGING CORPORATE EDUCATION IN CHINA

The entry of Mars into China in the early 1990s is an example of the strength of its education philosophy and the effectiveness of its program delivery.[4] It is also an example of how education initiatives helped the company to adapt to local circumstances. When the Mars manufacturing facility opened in Beijing in 1993, it very quickly became apparent that long-term success would be highly dependent on a workforce capable of operating under difficult, challenging and – in China – unknown conditions. Hence, fundamental to Mars success was the ability to educate new associates in China. The company would have to develop both an infrastructure and teaching capability to ensure that its associates could carry out their work properly. There was a need for further education not only in the areas of production and sales, but also in marketing, distribution, management, and leadership. As more professional and managerial education became a necessity, Mars invested further in the development of a formal education program, culminating in the formation of the "Mars Academy in China" in 2003. A year later the Mars China Graduate Development Program was launched.

The results were considered outstanding by both company executives and those who benefited from the education program, in particular Mars associates. The company benefited from associates with a higher level of skills than that of their competitors, as well as the level of certainty provided from the associated loyalty and longevity with the company, which delivered a long-term future for Mars in the region. Associates benefited from access to knowledge in areas that previously were not available to them. This in turn provided them with well-defined career paths and employment security, which in that country at that time was also quite difficult to obtain. Now, Mars benefits from a strong market share in China, estimated to be in the vicinity of 40 percent.[5]

The primary objective for all learning and development programs throughout that period would have been formed within a strategic environment that had an inward focus, i.e., a focus on building international presence through the delivery of high-quality products for global markets. The imperative was to retain cost competitiveness while also building competencies in the somewhat difficult task of manufacturing the heat-sensitive, perishable product that is chocolate.

Mars strategy and Mars University (2004–9)

The journey of strategic restructuring and renewal at Mars commenced in 2004 – following the appointment of Paul S. Michaels as its president. *Time* magazine published an interview that management consultant Howard Guttman held with Michaels not long after his appointment. Of interest in particular is this observation[6] of his:

> When Paul Michaels became president of Mars Inc. in 2004, he knew that the company needed to achieve far greater growth and financial return. But he faced internal organizational challenges.... The top team at Mars was siloed and replete with unspoken agendas. Members did not see the benefit of working as a team; they were only concerned with the success of their own region. There was some infighting, but mostly people just left one another alone.

Mars' long-standing philosophy of recruiting from within meant that it had few associates with experience in managing the newly established profit centers (segments) that resulted from corporate restructuring. This shortage contributed to the need to establish a corporate university enabling associates to acquire the necessary management and leadership capabilities, while protecting the consistency and strength of the Mars brand and its unique culture. Moreover, the Mars transformation agenda came to focus very much on the realization of efficiency and the restoration of competitiveness against other similarly global industry participants that included Kraft Foods, Cadbury Chocolate, Hershey's, and Nestlé.

Established in 2005, the first iteration of Mars University was grounded in a strategic focus on realization of an enhanced, strengthened and unique Mars culture, reinvigoration of the firm's values embodied in the Five Principles, and renewed attention to operating efficiency and effectiveness. Restructuring and efficiency also applied to the training activities within Mars, which were fragmented across the company and across the globe. The establishment of a Mars corporate university saw the consolidation of education initiatives, implemented through a uniform learning mechanism distributed to the Mars business units as a means of supporting individual country programs where appropriate. Content was focused on operational performance and capability development. The training programs resulted in a significant reduction in costs for the company, and according to Jon Shepherd, then chief learning officer, the overall benefit was:

> to get a competitive edge, using learning to meet business challenges and provide consistency around the world in an efficient manner.

Building on the synergies realized by a long period of restructuring and renewal, Mars was positioned much better to return to a broader strategic spectrum and a foray into an agenda of strategies for growth in 2009.

In line with the strategic priorities of the company, the design of the second iteration of Mars Corporate University was the direct result of a new strategic emphasis that was now focused on growth and continual organizational transformation and renewal. The thrust of Mars University this time around was to encompass *all* of the Five Principles, putting them into action in a more consistent way. To facilitate the change in strategic emphasis, Mars sought a uniform, companywide and integrated corporate university, one that was consistent with the corporate philosophy of "One Mars", to be relaunched under the banner of "A Single Mars University Experience."

Towards One Mars University

The program that sought to define the parameters of a newly designed corporate university had to compete with a number of other strategic change agendas that were vying for senior executive attention. An aggressive acquisition program was underway, the consolidation of the organization into global segments had commenced, and the standardization of business processes had begun. Mars had well and truly embarked on a journey to reinvent itself.

A reinvented company, it was thought, had to be led by a reinvented leadership, especially in a business that was in the habit of behaving differently than other similarly styled organizations. Effective outcomes from a redesigned education capability, it was considered, were surely the most efficient and effective way of delivering this requirement. As with the Mars entry into China, reliance on recruitment from outside the company was not really an option.

A reinvented Mars Corporate University would also be one of the key drivers of consolidation that would unite associates – on a global scale. In short, it was suggested that a One Mars strategy required a One Mars University. In tune with this sentiment, President Michaels announced that a strategic review of their existing university capabilities would be undertaken, to determine what needed to change, how and when it would be changed and most importantly, what a new Mars Corporate University would look like. Led by a senior Mars learning executive, Andre Martin, the Mars University leadership team was asked to identify how an internal education capability could be enhanced to ensure it could offer "more impact." Specifically, Andre Martin was being asked to design a corporate university that would:

provide world class programs to unleash the potential of Mars associates whilst reflecting the global nature of the business and embedding the Mars principles and culture.[7]

Illustrative of the confidence that Mars had in its university associates, the review was announced just at the time when many other corporations were looking to reduce their investments in education due to the global economic downturn that had recently taken hold. The underlying guidelines for the review were based on four objectives:

- Put the (internal) consumer first by creating an easy-to-access single university experience across regions and functions.
- Be a true partner to the business by creating stronger relationships within Mars University and across the business.
- Listen to our (internal) customers and design initiatives that impact business performance.
- Focus on the fundamentals by achieving excellence in the operational elements of a corporate university.

The corporate university review among other things included discussions with internal learning managers, the conduct of a customer satisfaction survey that included 3,100 associates, a statistical analysis of Mars online data, an internal cost and resource review, and interviews with leaders representing every segment and geographic location. Completed in March 2010, the review found:

- duplication and variation in global and local programming,
- lack of governance and integration, which contributed to inconsistencies and inefficiencies in budgeting, planning, reporting, design, and development processes,
- a funding model in line with industry average, but one that could not effectively respond to emerging business needs,
- a large number of instructor-led programs that resulted in a high cost per delivered hour vs. benchmark companies, at the expense of applied and self-directed learning,
- uncertainty among associates as to who Mars University was for,
- less than 30 percent of the associates able to agree with the statement that Mars University contributed to business goals, impacted job performance, responded to changing needs, and produced cost-effective results.

Although the review identified deficiencies in many of Mars University's "operational" areas, these were accepted as issues that could be readily addressed through restructuring as well as organizational and process redesign. At a higher level, the review concluded that Mars University needed to realign itself to the direction in which the corporate strategy was going – way beyond a tweaking around the edges of cost management and control. It was up to Mars University to deliver. To do so would require a wholesale transformation from the role as provider of functional expertise and services designed to assist with improvements in productivity to that of an all encompassing education facility. Key goals would be to empower and inspire (realizing potential and making a difference for individuals, the Mars business, and the planet), and to be a committed ally (making a positive impact as a dedicated partner sharing associates' goals). Soon, Mars University unveiled a new look and feel encapsulated in the belief that "the sky is the limit, so set your sights high: we'll help you get there." The new look of Mars University is now a corporate university comprising ten functional colleges (e.g., Finance, Sales, Supply, Corporate Affairs) and one cross-functional college (Leadership). Content provided by these colleges is made accessible across the globe and provides a set of resources and learning methods in the form of training courses, e-learning modules, a library, and a research facility. At Mars University, the college curricula are created by top Mars associates, supported by external experts.

Transformation plans and actions

A new corporate university management team was announced in November 2010, and the objective of their first meeting was to develop a game plan leading to the realization of a redesigned Mars Corporate University embedded as a business partner in the six segments of the company. Its expected role was to exert a strong influence on the change in strategic direction of the entire company. The development and design steps taken – called work streams – are depicted in Figure 5.2. They include elements of both the corporate university business system (value propositions) and the organizational system (management systems).

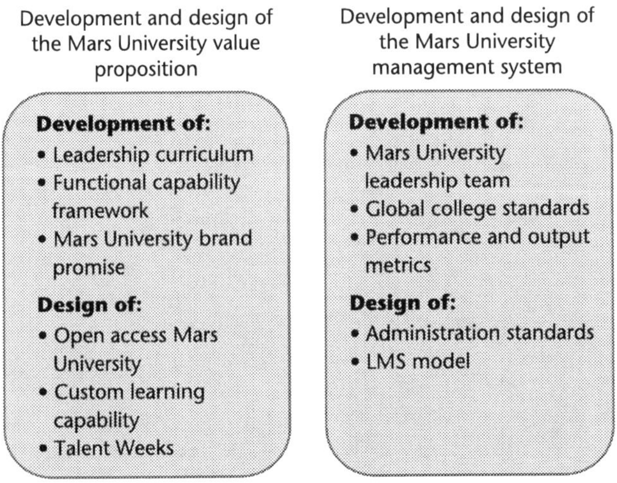

Development and design of the Mars University value proposition	Development and design of the Mars University management system
Development of: • Leadership curriculum • Functional capability framework • Mars University brand promise **Design of:** • Open access Mars University • Custom learning capability • Talent Weeks	**Development of:** • Mars University leadership team • Global college standards • Performance and output metrics **Design of:** • Administration standards • LMS model

FIGURE 5.2 Work streams for Mars University development

Source: Analysis by the authors

The Mars University development and transformation plan was centered on six specific tenets of success (see Figure 5.3), each designed to improve the efficiency and effectiveness of the corporate university *and* accelerate the Mars strategy. The six tenets of success cover the following characteristics, actions, and results:

- *Strengthen senior leadership capability.* Mars managers are helped to develop the skills they need, to ensure that every associate at Mars has a world-class line manager. The 70-20-10 learning rule[8] is followed here.
  - Action: A Leadership Development Program was launched. Mars University introduced Leadership@Mars, a series of iconic programs for all managers from front line to senior leader (see Exhibit 5.2).
  - Result: The launch of Leadership@Mars ensured that all line managers are introduced to the same content that will help Mars to build a corporate culture where line managers are fully committed to taking primary responsibility for the development of their people.
- *Develop a globally aligned approach for the Mars Functional Colleges.* Mars University consumers can locate and participate in the same learning programs worldwide.
  - Action: Apart from the global Mars University brand launch, actions here include the establishment of a set of global standards that align Mars University functional colleges.
  - Results: With the alignment of Mars functional colleges, associates grow more easily within or across functions. Moreover, the alignment allowed a rollout of foundational training in every functional college across the organization. As a result of the alignments, use of the Mars University resources by Mars associates increased five-fold.
- *Provide access to a single university experience.* Mars University provides access to all associates, no matter where they are in the world or which Mars functional college they attend, and regardless of the region or function.
  - Action: Development of a functional capability framework with the purpose of bringing all Mars colleges together, using the same consistent development framework and language. The ten functional colleges of Mars University have begun to work with a standard curriculum, which builds the skills and capabilities of associates in alignment with each segment's business level strategy.
  - Results: Every Mars associate receives materials of the highest standard from Mars University. All functional colleges and curricula are presented in one global brochure, and all associates have access to a "functional capability framework" that uses a consistent language to highlight development opportunities and metrics across the business.
- *Achieve Operational Excellence.* The corporate university should operate systems and processes supporting one Mars University.
  - Action: Introduction of an enterprise-wide learning management system[9] (LMS) to offer combinations of instructor-led classroom training, self-paced eLearning, and virtual classes.

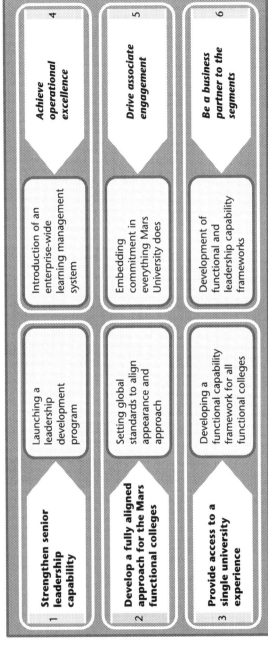

FIGURE 5.3 Overview of six Mars tenets of success and actions

Source: Analysis by the authors

EXHIBIT 5.2: OVERVIEW OF MARS UNIVERSITY LEADERSHIP DEVELOPMENT PROGRAMS

As a result of the actions taken in 2010, the company saw the introduction of many new Mars University programs. An example is the Mars Leadership Development program. Focus areas for this program are an appreciation and understanding of Mars' Five Principles, the development of leadership capabilities as well as the sharing of ideas and best practices amongst peer groups. Launched in three phases, Phase 1 was first tried in January 2011. It is an entry level program that focuses on the foundation of leadership. Phase 1 coursework is designed to equip new line managers with the necessary knowledge and sufficient skill to enhance the commitment and performance of every associate. At this introductory level, the Mars objective is to accelerate the development and performance of specific groups of associates, such as high-potential associates, line managers and general managers. Course content typically includes presentations from senior leaders who are invited to provide insight into their perspective of the skills required to succeed in the business. Phase 2 of the program was launched in January 2012, designed to strengthen the skills and abilities of experienced line managers. Phase 3 was first piloted in 2013, designed to train mid-level leaders to apply creative and analytical skills to solve increasingly difficult business challenges.

From there, Associates at senior leadership levels have the opportunity to participate in other courses. Two examples of these are *"Mars Leadership at the Peak"*, and *"Leading in Unprecedented Times"*. The *"Mars Leadership at the Peak"* course is designed to give senior leaders an opportunity to better understand the strengths and areas for development in their personal leadership style. This program helps to motivate leaders and explore the legacy they want to create. *"Leading in Unprecedented Times"* focuses on the key debates, tensions and strategic choices facing Mars in the future. Topics include investments in sustainability, maintaining a successful business, and balancing the need for consistent operations with local needs. It provides management teams with the opportunity to apply lessons learned through discussions of case studies.

- o Results: The Mars University management team members are now in a position to deliver a significantly stronger alignment to the business.
- *Drive Associate Engagement.* Realization of the dream espoused by the founding father Forrest Mars, Sr. "to ensure that this thing called Mars is a source of happiness and a better way of life" through Mars University education programs.
  - o Action: Enabling all segments to benefit from equal access to the offerings of Mars University without the need for central support.

o   Results: Commitment is embedded in everything that Mars University does, through the way they teach, the way they interact with line managers, and the way they offer courses to their associates.
- *Be a business partner to the segments.* All associates know the skills required for being successful at Mars, and Mars University will provide the required learning opportunities to build capability and respond to emerging business needs.
  o   Action: All Mars associates have the opportunity to extend and develop individual skills in their specialist functions and areas of management and leadership.
  o   Results: Mars Corporate University brings to life a belief that learning agility enables an associate to have a career that spans multiple segments, geographies, and functions. Frameworks used in the learning process also provide managers with a tool to aid their performance review discussions. Associates understand all of the capabilities – functional and leadership – to succeed in their role and the possibilities for development.

The Customized Learning Group

In addition to the plans and actions for transformation, the corporate university management team has formed a new unit called the Customized Learning Group. This unit consists of four dedicated members, and it serves as the innovation arm of the corporate university. The unit is charged with the task of seeking trends, assessing needs and delivering interventions to address business challenges that are not fully covered by the standard curriculum.

As an example, in 2010 a problem was identified in the newly formed global petcare segment at Mars. Despite an investment of over 40 years in pet science at the Waltham Centre for Petcare Nutrition (WCPN), it appeared that the scientific basis and knowledge of the Mars petcare specific products was not well understood. Specifically there was little appreciation about the reason for their formulations, the quality of raw materials used, and so on. Even worse, evidence was found that some associates actually believed the myths they had heard or read about on the internet. Such myths included accusations that Mars used fillers in its ingredients that were not good for pets, that poor quality meat was used, and that "home made is best." As explained by Mars, the facts are that the products of the company are scientifically designed to be "complete and balanced" using micro quantities of ingredients that when manufactured provides nutrition far superior to any home-made food leading to better pet health, wellbeing, and longevity.

These misconceptions were particularly critical in – though not limited to – customer-focused functions such as sales, marketing, and corporate affairs, as well as certain emerging geographies. It hampered the company's ability to change adverse rumor-based perceptions held by external partners and key influencers, and this in turn resulted in lost sales.

The Customized Learning Group was asked to co-lead the development of a "Petcare Academy" offering basic, advanced, and expert level education for Mars associates. The role of the Group was to deliver the work using best practice approaches and design principles from Mars University, and establish a sustainable delivery structure within Mars Petcare. Over time every new associate would receive the basic training upon joining the company, and the existing 27,000 associates would be informed better as time allowed.

To make the Petcare Academy work, the Customized Learning Group teamed up with WCPN experts early in 2011. Starting with a basic module, a pilot project was conducted in North America with a combination of new as well as re-purposed content from WCPN. At the end of April the basic module was piloted for a group of 35 associates in workshop format. This was then rolled out to Brazil and Japan, and adapted to a group format of 200 participants to be employed in North America. During 2012 the roll-out continued and resulted in the formation of train-the-trainer events, the conduct of quarterly alignments, the establishment of key performance metrics and the establishment and deployment of a "champions" network, followed by the introduction of a commitment champions community webinar. In addition, advanced modules were launched in Petcare Academy branding, the bulk of this being re-purposed and edited content that extended availability to those working outside of the WCPN R&D function. By the end of 2012, no less than 10,000 associates had received education on the petcare segment from the newly established Petcare Academy.

Today, support from the Customized Learning Group to the Petcare Academy continues on an ad hoc consultancy basis. In parallel the unit has taken what was learned from the approach in Petcare, and applied it to other segment academies, tailored to the specific needs of the chewing gum, confectionery, and food businesses globally.

Lessons learned

Mars is on a journey of transforming the learning function, proud to offer a model that other corporate universities[10] can follow. As explained by Andre Martin, chief learning officer at Mars, a number of lessons were learned along the way that will continue to support the ongoing transformation initiatives at Mars University. In particular, this corporate university will continue to focus its strategy exclusively on what makes the most impact to the business in alignment with the stated objectives outlined in the review of 2010.

Four of these objectives stand out:

- *Put our consumers first.* Create easy-to-access, consistent learning experiences across regions and functions that help associates solve our critical business challenges.
- *Be a true partner to the business.* Listen to our business customers and design initiatives that impact business performance.
- *Continue to focus on the fundamentals.* Achieve excellence in the operational elements of a corporate university.
- *Less is more.* Aim for fewer, but better programs.

Looking back, looking ahead

Mars University helped to orient company strategies towards the realization of higher returns, transformation to one integrated company, and engagement in the challenge of addressing major societal issues related to food. Mars University did this by nurturing the company culture, ensuring world-class line management, providing associates with the functional skills needed, and by helping every associate to "Make Mars Mean More." Mars as a company has reaped the benefits from deliberate use of organizational learning as a means to turn ideas and inspiration into results, and to empower associates to enhance their individual performance levels.

As a private, family-owned company, Mars is not subject to the quarterly reporting and performance criteria that are typically found in publicly listed companies. According to President Michaels, Mars thinks in terms of generations, not quarterly returns. They can therefore afford to take a long-term view when making investments in their corporate university, doing the job properly and building greater substance and drive as the organizational transformation program picks up pace. From a Mars perspective, Mars University is still in its infancy, but satisfied that its transformation has touched every aspect of the way the corporate university and indeed the company works. As President Michaels put it:

> We are starting slow – getting our strategy, resources and organization right – to finish fast. We are just at the beginning of the learning transformation. During the next three to five years, Mars University will continue to implement its strategy.

Michaels sums up the Mars ambitions for the future as follows:

> Addressing the challenges that we share with society is part of our mandate as a food company committed to making a difference. The issues are global, complex and fast-changing, so our response must be sophisticated and of equal scale. Our Five Principles – Quality, Responsibility, Mutuality, Efficiency, and Freedom – have always guided the kind of company we are, and we believe that remaining dedicated to them will ensure our business has a lasting positive effect on the world.

Mars University will have a strong influence on that ambition. The momentum and leadership capability the corporate university is building is increasingly turning organizational learning within Mars from one of support for change to that of a driver of change. When that happens, Mars University will be a key provider of inputs to the strategic decision making process: an initiator of strategic thinking across organizational barriers and, ultimately, an instigator of organizational transformation and renewal. Being a corporate university that wants to mean more to Mars, Mars University is likely to raise the bar and reinvent itself once again.

Notes

1. With this statement, Michaels points to a World Health Organization publication from 2011, which estimates that there are one billion obese people in the world, while at the same time two billion people are undernourished because they lack access to adequate food supplies.
2. Forrest E. Mars, Sr. in 1932 issued a resolve that the Mars Company would exhibit the characteristics of a responsible, caring, and generous employer. This commitment was subsequently articulated in 1947 as the company objective of "creating a mutuality of benefits for all stakeholders."
3. Within the company, the employees of Mars, Inc. are all called "associates."
4. Source: Allen, L. L. (2010) *Chocolate Fortunes*, Wiley Periodicals (Jan/Feb).
5. Nieburg, O. (2011), Chocolate Driving Growth in Chinese Confectionery Market. confectionerynews.com.
6. Guttman, H. M. (2009), A Lesson Straight from Mars. *Time*, 29 January.
7. This quote is taken from a submission for a Chief Learning Officer (CLO) of the Year award. Mars senior management was so satisfied with the outcome of its redesigned corporate university that they nominated Andre Martin and his colleagues for special awards. As a result, Jim Brodie, director of operations at Mars University, was awarded silver in the Business Impact Division of the CLO award program in 2012.
8. The 70 percent self-directed, 20 percent classroom, 10 percent application rule is a learning and development logic derived from research by Michael M. Lombardo and Robert W. Eichinger (2000).
9. Mars set strict criteria for software selection, which included ease of use, application to organizations the size of Mars, configuration capability (at minimal cost of customization), and a partnership approach that matched Mars' needs and culture, which they describe as a business relationship for success. A final requirement was for the software to incorporate a strong "informal learning" capability.
10. Mars University received such awards as Best Corporate University Launch in 2006, Excellence in Business Alignment (2006, 2007, 2010), and Excellence in Leadership (2010). In 2010, Mars received the Great Workplace Award. In 2011, Mars Russia was recognized as one of the three best companies for developing leaders.

Literature

Allen, L.L. (2010) *Chocolate Fortunes*, Wiley Periodicals, Inc., Jan/Feb.
Corporate University Exchange (2008). *The Secret to Mars Corporation's Success (And it's Not Chocolate)*. New York: Corporate University Exchange.
Guttman, H.M. (2009). A Lesson Straight from Mars. *Time*, Thursday, January 29.
Kaplan, D.A. (2013). 100 Best Companies to Work For. Mars Inc.: A pretty sweet place to work, *Fortune*, February 4.
Lombardo, M.M. and R.W. Eichinger (2000). High Potentials as High Learners. *Human Resource Management*. Vol. 39, No. 4, pp. 321–30.
Mars, F. (2008). *The Historical Society of Oak Park and River Forest*. http://www.oprf.com/oprfhist/marsf.htm (retrieved 2008-02-25).
Senge, P.M. (1990). *The Fifth Discipline: The Art and Practice of the Learning Organization*. London: Random House.

6

DELOITTE UNIVERSITY: DEVELOPING AS ONE[1]

Co-authors: Nick van Dam and Bill Pelster

> To grow the world's best leaders
> —*Vision Deloitte University*

It is through learning that companies adapt to their ever-changing environment. For companies in the professional services industry, learning simply is a sine qua non. Just to keep up with the rapid change of pace is already a challenge, let alone shaping the environment. As in most things that are hard to execute and ambiguous in nature but critical to get right, Deloitte[2] considers learning and leadership development as one of its strategic spearheads. Deloitte University is the tool that shapes the professional skills for the organization.

This chapter will provide an overview of Deloitte, its strategy, and the role that learning and leadership development plays in the execution of its strategy. The chapter will end with lessons learned and key challenges for the future.

About Deloitte

Deloitte is the brand under which over more than 193,000 professionals in independent firms throughout the world collaborate to provide audit, consulting, financial advisory, risk management, and tax services. The establishment of Deloitte can be traced back to 1849 in London, when William Welch Deloitte was appointed the first independent auditor in history. In 1880, the first overseas office opened in New York. Deloitte grew from a pure play accounting firm into an integrated professional services organization, structured around four separate business subsidiaries: audit and enterprise risk services, tax, consulting, and financial advisory services. Deloitte grew both organically and by acquisition. For example, when Arthur Andersen (a global professional services firm) collapsed in 2002 in the aftermath of

TABLE 6.1 Number of people employed at Deloitte, breakdown per region

The Americas	84,855
Europe, Middle East, and Africa	68,317
Asia Pacific	40,187

Source: Deloitte Touche Tohmatsu Limited 2012 Global Report

the Enron scandal, Deloitte hired a large number of their people. Deloitte also acquired companies with very specific services, like the strategy consulting firm the Monitor Group and Bersin & Associates in 2012.

Each Deloitte member firm provides services in a particular geographic area and is subject to the rules of the countries in which it operates. In fiscal year 2012, Deloitte employed 193,359 people in 48 member firms operating in 153 different countries and regions (see Table 6.1). Aggregate annual revenues hit the US$31.3 billion mark in fiscal year 2012 and the aggregate growth rate of the Deloitte member firms went up by 8.6 percent.

Deloitte's strategy

Complexity and rapid change are defining and permanent features of the landscape for Deloitte's clients and Deloitte's business. Deloitte's ability to fulfill its promise to its clients and sustain its growth rest on executing a strategy that appropriately addresses a fluid competitive environment and anticipates the current and future needs of clients around the world.

In 2011, Deloitte developed a four-year business strategy, known as the "As One Strategy," with the ambition to emerge as the undisputed global leader in professional services. This strategic plan outlines which professional services in different markets will be offered to Deloitte's clients. The Deloitte Network is capitalizing on market opportunities through four strategic choices:

- *Market Leadership:* Creating or sustaining a leadership position in each key market Deloitte serves by anticipating and rapidly responding to changing market realities and consistently outperforming the competition.
- *Focused market investments:* Growing and expanding the business especially in high-growth strategic markets.
- *Operate globally:* With the scope of the Deloitte member firm structure, focusing on operating more globally, while ensuring consistent, high-quality client service.
- *As One:* Strengthen the professional services Deloitte delivers by working across geographic, functional, and business borders.

The "As One Strategy" reflects the efforts and energy of thousands of member firm partners and professionals who participated in surveys, working sessions, and project teams to shape its content. Deloitte Touche Tohmatsu Limited (DTTL) Global CEO Barry Salzberg summarized the new strategy as follows:

> For an organization to reach its ultimate potential, it must understand how its clients and its people define success, and then respond as a leader, always demonstrating its ability to create and add value. And it must do this seamlessly, throughout the world.

Deloitte University

Deloitte needs strong leaders who can leverage new perspectives and learn to better address complex and critical situations – from addressing sustainability and global competitiveness issues to fostering innovation and creativity. The US member firm's response to this challenge is Deloitte University (DU), a US$300 million investment to create and sustain a new approach to leadership development. Deloitte University opened in October 2011 on a 107-acre campus near Dallas, Texas. The vision for Deloitte University is "To grow the world's best leaders." The goal of Deloitte University is to develop strong, globally-minded leaders for today and a pipeline of leaders for tomorrow. It is a catalyst for leadership and lifelong learning – where Deloitte professionals at all levels connect, share their best thinking, and identify and capitalize on new and innovative ideas and approaches. Deloitte University has transformed learning across the organization with action learning, simulations, leader-led experiences, interactive technology, customized development, and social learning.

The faculty is deeply-talented with most courses delivered by Deloitte member firm leaders. The DU premises include environmentally-conscious designed classrooms, guest rooms, an amphitheater, Board Room Suite, and a wellness/fitness center. Learning technologies include satellite-linked tele-classrooms, high-definition tele-suites for global instruction and conferencing, and a Cyber Center with the latest in technology for social networking.

Since 2011, DU has run an innovative senior manager milestone program to help prepare new leaders for their roles, responsibilities, and continued development. The program features simulations, coaching, and live events. At the Lead Client Service Partner (LCSP) level, leaders pursue an integrated approach to learning and development. Deloitte member firm professionals around the world have access to the Deloitte Learning Platform including web-based training, recorded webinars, web-apps, e-books, podcasts, learning videos, games, and simulations. This will provide them with on-demand learning which is available at any time and any place.

Since 2012, DU has organized an annual global new partner seminar, attended by 400+ new partners and principles from all Deloitte member firms around the world. The program provides attendees with opportunities to share knowledge and build on their experience and reinforce a global development culture.

By the end of 2012, Deloitte University has realized:

- 40,000+ professionals attending DU from 70 countries
- 1 million+ live learning hours
- 20 industry sectors represented
- 90+ percent of delivery done by Deloitte people.

DTTL Global CEO, Barry Salzberg initiated and championed Deloitte University while serving in his previous role as Deloitte US CEO. He believes Deloitte University will allow the Deloitte organization to: "Instill our values in our people through learning and development," which he believes is critical to Deloitte's long-term success.

Education Permanente at Deloitte University

From new hires to CEOs, people across Deloitte are enabled to continually enhance their skills. Efforts are made by DU to achieve higher levels of consistency in the curricula, content, standards, and branding across Deloitte globally. To achieve this, learning standards are introduced (among others based on benchmarking, performance measurement, and accreditation) and conversations are held with the Deloitte member firms.

Deloitte member firm professionals around the world have access to nearly 50,000 digital learning elements that are available 24×7 via the Deloitte Learning Platform including web-based training, recorded webinars, web-apps, e-books, podcasts, learning videos, games, and simulations. This will provide them with on-demand learning which is available at any time and any place.

Learning curricula for technical, industry, professional, and leadership learning can be accessed through the Deloitte Learning Platform. The platform, as depicted in Figure 6.1, is also used for registration and administration of all learning events which are organized by the member firms. Deloitte Professionals have access to their personal learning plan and all completed learning will be stored in people's online learning history. The Deloitte Virtual Classroom, hosted on the Deloitte Learning Platform, is an online virtual learning environment that enables highly interactive classroom learning. It creates a collaborative virtual experience, in real-time, so that participants feel connected to each other and to their facilitator.

Talent Strategy definition and execution requires people with diverse skill sets. In addition to an internal team of learning and development professionals, Deloitte engages specialists and senior project managers from the Human Capital practices. Deloitte uses well-tested principles of project management, stakeholder management, and change management for all initiates which need to be implemented. Moreover, state of the art insights from research on learning – such as brain-based learning as described more in detail in Exhibit 6.1 – are used to refresh and redesign learning and leadership curricula.

Courses

2,100,000+ Courses taken in 47 different member firms

4,100 Courses available in 15 languages other than English

3,200 Harvard Business Publishing certification courses completed

Online

15,000 Online courses

25,000 Books online

56,000 Professionals attended over 5,100 virtual sessions

Benchmark achievements

3 New industry curricula

4 New industry learning guides

FIGURE 6.1   The Deloitte Learning Platform

Source: Adapted from Deloitte Touche Tohmatsu Limited 2012 Global Report

---

EXHIBIT 6.1: BRAIN-BASED LEARNING AT DELOITTE

The Deloitte University learning and leadership curricula go through ongoing stages of refreshment and redesign. One of the key trends is that DU increasingly utilizes brain-based learning practices. For example:

1. Classroom programs are designed to support a high level of engagement and intentionally touch on emotions. It is expected that learners participate actively by collaborating, elaborating, verbalizing, drawing, and sharing what has been learned. Lecture-driven experiences are kept to a minimum.
2. Learning sessions are shortened in duration and provide a high level of personalization through a typical 5:1 student facilitator ratio.
3. Participants are encouraged to use valuable offsite classroom time to reflect on one's development. It is actively discouraged to look at email/text during classroom time, making sure that people stay focused on learning.
4. A large inventory of digital learning facilities provides people with an opportunity to acquire knowledge and develop skills as needed. New skills can be applied directly on-the-job, making the learning "stick."
5. At Deloitte University in Dallas, health and wellbeing are supported by fitness and yoga/meditation classes. Participants can also take advantage of healthy food choices and personal fitness assessments to stimulate body and brain.

Deloitte University and the As One strategy

The Deloitte learning strategy is derived from the Deloitte As One strategy. A number of "As One" strategic priorities are supported by Deloitte University, including: build deep industry knowledge; be an innovation catalyst; expand sustainability services; investments in audit quality; and borderless development, and will be described in more detail below.

Build deep industry knowledge. DU has created a global and consistent industry learning curriculum to deepen industry knowledge of the professionals working at the Deloitte member firms. A global learning program supports the improvement of member firms' capabilities through a common foundation based on three pillars:

1. *Competencies.* A clear definition of the skills and knowledge required for practitioners to be industry proficient, at a global level;
2. *Curriculum.* A laddered path to proficiency for a given industry, starting with foundation, including cross-industry as well as by industry or sector specific learning;
3. *Proficiency.* Measured levels that define competencies at three levels so that member firms can identify what skill-sets reside where.

A total of 165 industry learning courses providing basic foundation industry knowledge are available for industries (and the sectors within) for: Consumer Business, Energy & Resources, Financial Services, Life Sciences & Health Care, Manufacturing, Public Sector, Technology, and Media & Telecommunications.

Be an innovation catalyst. Business Analytics is a fast growing business that Deloitte invests in significantly. To support Deloitte professionals' capability, a Deloitte Analytics curriculum has been launched covering the core analytic themes of the organization: Information Management, Performance Optimization, and Analytic Insights. According to Tim Phillipps, DTTL Leader Analytics:

> Central to the development of this curriculum is the principle that we should provide practitioners across the organization with a common learning experience. Among other outcomes, promoting a degree of consistency will help to ensure member firms' analytics practitioners have the same baseline knowledge of analytics tools, techniques, and approaches, and, as a consequence, that these practitioners can more readily be deployed seamlessly and globally.

This analytics curriculum has been designed by learning professionals in collaboration with business leaders and subject-matter specialists. A blend of learning modalities has been included in this curriculum.

Expand sustainability services. Over the next four years, Deloitte will invest millions of dollars in sustainability services to help clients transition to sustainable business models and practices that will deliver top and bottom-line long-term growth. Recognizing its own responsibilities in the sustainability agenda, Deloitte measures its environmental performance, reports its societal engagement, and is defining goals and actions to generate improvements, particularly in the use of energy and resources. Learning programs have been designed to develop Deloitte colleagues in this important area.

Investments in audit quality. Deloitte is constructively engaged with regulators and other stakeholders worldwide on issues such as the role of the auditor and financial reporting, with significant emphasis on enhancing audit value and quality, improving corporate governance, and increasing public confidence in the audit process. Deloitte has launched "Deloitte Audit," a global transformative audit platform that provides clients with a customized approach to their most important issues and risks, and exemplifies Deloitte's commitment to audit quality. Deloitte has launched a number of programs to get its auditors up-to-date on this platform.

Borderless development. Leveraging the power of a borderless network also means identifying and tapping the strengths of people everywhere. To serve cross-border clients, Deloitte runs a mobility program whereby member firms contribute to and tap talent. In fiscal year 2012, mobility assignments increased 21 percent from the previous year: Nearly 5,300 Deloitte member firm people were on short and long-term assignments designed to transfer skills and capabilities, develop globally-minded leaders, and better serve cross-border clients. Deloitte University plays a critical role in preparing leaders for international assignments through programs like attending Global Lead Client Service Partner Program which focuses on their new international role and specific competencies.

Deloitte University program governance structure

At DTTL DU program decisions are made based on facts and through extensive collaboration with large groups of stakeholders. It is important that everybody has been heard and different options have been considered. Extensive consultation does lead to better decision making and supports a smooth implementation of the strategy. In order to organize stakeholders' involvement, DTTL has established a Global Learning Council and a Global Talent Council which reports to the DTTL Executive. The councils include professional leaders from the ten largest Deloitte member firms and are chaired by the DTTL Global Leaders for Talent and Learning & Development. The councils play a significant role in building support for execution, among others through collaborating on defining key initiatives.

Lessons learned

1. Learning about yourself and the culture of the organization requires the right combination of digital learning and physical classroom learning because this

creates the opportunity to connect with people and enhance the culture and reinforce the values of the organization.
2. In an increasing virtual and digital world it is key to have a place – like Deloitte University in Dallas – where people have a shared common experience and spend time in problem solving, deep skill development, and reflection.
3. The ownership of the talent agenda by senior leadership. The DTTL Global CEO, Barry Salzberg, is a supporter and sponsor of leadership development at Deloitte. Deloitte University has been built based on his vision of culture and learning in a large, complex organization.
4. Because Deloitte has a workforce dispersed over more than 153 countries and regions, diversity needs to be represented in the global governance bodies. It is important to collect input from colleagues from all over the world. Moreover, member firms differ in size and represent different cultures; therefore it is important to be respectful of their need to localize some programs. With that in mind, the core design of Deloitte simulations allows for easy localization.
5. It is essential to develop deep and respectful relationships with different stakeholders. Regular meetings are necessary. In a large and complex organization like Deloitte one can hardly "over-communicate" to stakeholders to gain and retain support.

Conclusions and looking ahead

Professional development at Deloitte is of great importance. People always need to be well-trained and up-to-date in their field. But that is not enough. To sustain its leading position in the professional services industry, Deloitte is closely following (and many times creating) trends relevant to customers. Deloitte University has been established to stay abreast in an industry characterized by a very short knowledge "half time."

Deloitte member firms will continue to execute on the "As One Strategy." As part of this, Deloitte expects to increase its total workforce to 250,000 professionals by fiscal year 2015. In tune to this need, the Global Learning and Leadership Strategy consist of four pillars. The first pillar is "Develop the next generation of leaders." The aim is to provide the depth and diversity of talent required for Deloitte's global growth strategy. Deloitte University has created a common leader development framework for multiple levels. This framework is supported by the development and deployment of a curriculum of leadership programs for member firm partners and principles. The second pillar revolves around "Designing and delivering a global DU curriculum." Deloitte needs to develop leading professionals who have consistent skills and deep knowledge in technical, industry, professional, and leadership in a cost-effective way. DU aims to develop a consistent global Deloitte University Curriculum including both classroom learning as well as digital learning. Depending on the program, the classroom learning can be delivered globally, regionally, or nationally/locally. The third pillar is to "Achieve agility through technology." The aim is to leverage new and existing technologies to enable the internal learning department to meet the speed of change that member firms require in the most efficient way possible. Manage the digital content catalogue by continually assessing the quality and quantity of the content. Maximize and enhance the offerings from vendors like Harvard Business Publishing. Increase delivery through mobile devices such as smartphones and tablets using apps, videos, games, simulations, ebooks, webinars, virtual classrooms, and assessments. Provide rapid mobile learning development tools for conversion of existing learning into mobile learning. Enhance and execute on a learning technologies roadmap which will provide Deloitte people with a leading Learning Platform. The fourth pillar of the Global Learning and Leadership Strategy is concerned with "Learning shared services." Currently, the Deloitte Learning Platform administration is supported by the Deloitte Learning Shared Services Function. DU has started to expand shared services with Deloitte Virtual Classroom administration and facilitation support, e-content sourcing services, Digital Learning development services, and learning administration services.

The Deloitte learning strategy is derived from the Deloitte As One strategy. Developing the next generation of leaders, designing and delivering a global DU curriculum, achieving agility through technology, and the expansion of learning shared services will shape corporate learning at Deloitte in the coming years.

Notes

1 This chapter contains general information only and Deloitte is not, by means of this publication, rendering accounting, business, financial, investment, legal, tax, or other professional advice or services. This chapter is not a substitute for such professional advice or services, nor should it be used as a basis for any decision or action that may affect your business. Before making any decision or taking any action that may affect your business, you should consult a qualified professional advisor. Deloitte shall not be responsible for any loss sustained by any person who relies on this chapter.
2 Deloitte refers to one or more of Deloitte Touche Tohmatsu Limited, a UK private company limited by guarantee, and its network of member firms, each of which is a legally separate and independent entity. Please see www.deloitte.com/about for a detailed description of the legal structure of Deloitte Touche Tohmatsu Limited and its member firms. Please see www.deloitte.com/us/about for a detailed description of the legal structure of Deloitte LLP and its subsidiaries. Certain services may not be available to attest clients under the rules and regulations of public accounting.

7

SHELL PROJECT ACADEMY: DEVELOPING A LEARNING COMMUNITY

Co-author: Hans Wierda

> We need four-star generals to lead our investment projects!
> Exclamation at the launch of the Shell Project Academy

Investing in the exploration of oil and gas reserves – in other words, looking for new oil wells and gas reservoirs – is vital for the long-term survival of any oil and gas company. They must continuously seek and find new reserves to replenish the sources from which they draw oil and gas as raw materials. Opportunities to explore for oil and gas reserves in any country are either directly or indirectly controlled by national governments, which exercise this control through their national oil companies or regulatory bodies. For Shell International, also known as Royal Dutch Shell, it is vital to be capable of convincing governments and any other potential business partners that this company can reliably deliver on investment portfolios for exploration projects. After all, Shell is no different from its competitors in vying for access to new reserves in the major resource holding countries. Moreover, maintaining production levels and replacing the productive reserves are two equally essential business activities at which the company must succeed in order to sustain investor community confidence.

The Shell Project Academy (SPA) was established in 2005 as part of a series of measures which were undertaken to revitalize the corporate strategy, aiming to re-establish a sustainable competitive position in the development of hydrocarbon reserves for business partners in the international oil and gas industry.[1] For the strategy to succeed, building and sustaining a large corps of managers with excellent project management capabilities was pivotal. In 2013, the Shell Project Academy is still actively engaged in continual replenishment of the company's reservoir of qualified project managers, to stay abreast of developments in the competitive energy sector with highest levels of competence in project management.

After a brief introduction to the oil and gas industry that follows here, key characteristics of what is known as the Shell "project world" will provide the context for a presentation of the Shell Project Academy design, development, and deployment within the company, as well as the lessons learned.

Shell in the international oil and gas industry

The international oil and gas industry is one of the largest in the world in terms of revenues, totaling US$ 4,370 billion in 2011. The total production of oil and gas companies in 2011 added up to 87.9 million barrels of oil, and 120.1 trillion cubic feet of natural gas.

Shell is one of the world's largest international companies active in every area of the oil, gas, and energy industry, including exploration and production, refining, distribution and marketing, petrochemicals, power generation, trading, and renewable energy. The top competitors of Shell are giants the like of Exxon Mobil, Chevron (both US-based), PetroChina, Petrobras (Brazil), Gazprom (Russia), BP (UK), and Total (France), only to mention the top eight oil and gas companies in the world. Figure 7.1 depicts these eight largest oil companies worldwide and their shares in an aggregate annual revenue worth more than US$ 229.5 billion in 2011. Annual capital investments of the eight largest companies in the oil and gas industry range from approximately US$ 23 billion to US$ 45 billion per year, with an upward trend due to the rising costs of exploration and development, because of the remote locations of yet unexploited reserves. With such high investments involved in the oil and gas industry, costs are high when projects underperform, get delayed, or even fail.

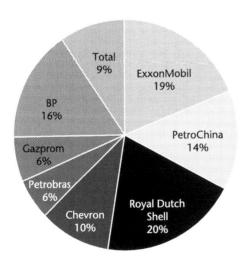

FIGURE 7.1 Top eight oil and gas companies in the world, with their relative shares in the aggregate annual revenue 2011

Source: Analysis by the authors[2,3,4]

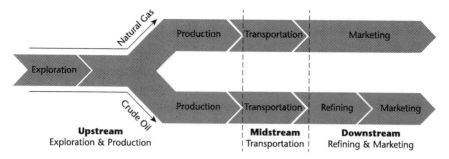

FIGURE 7.2 Upstream, midstream, and downstream activities in the oil and gas industry

Source: Analysis by the authors

It is common in the oil and gas industry to make a distinction between "upstream," "midstream," and "downstream" activities (as depicted in Figure 7.2). Upstream activities involve exploration projects aimed at finding new oil and gas reserves, and making newly found sources ready for production. Production, the extraction of oil and gas, is seen as an upstream activity too. Typical upstream assets include offshore production platforms, evacuation lines, and onshore oil and gas processing plants to allow transportation over long distances. Long-distance transportation, either by long trunk pipelines or by tanker, is often labeled as a midstream activity. Next, downstream business units add value to crude oil and gas by refining and using it as feedstock for fuels, lubricants (lube oil), and chemicals, or energy. The marketing of these products is also part of the downstream activities. Facilities in the downstream part of oil and gas companies include refineries, chemical plants, and any infrastructure supporting these facilities, such as power plants, roads, jetties, and ports.

Many smaller oil and gas companies are focused on their own country or region, while others have a wide international presence. Shell has operations in over 90 countries, almost equally distributed over all continents, producing approximately 3.1 million BOE/day,[5] operating 47 refineries, also selling fuel and petroleum products at 44,000 service and filling stations worldwide. Owing to a high degree of autonomy for local operating companies, the Shell workforce is characterized by a large degree of diversity in terms of cultural and social backgrounds, ethnic groups, gender, and nationality. Counting some 5,500 out of 90,000 people who work for the company, Shell is one of the largest commercial employers of senior-level expatriates in the world. Up to 40 percent of these "expats" originate from countries other than the UK and the Netherlands, which are the countries of origin of Shell. More than a quarter of the Shell employees come from outside Europe. Given the internationally diverse nature of its workforce and global presence, Shell is seen as one of the most multi-national companies in the world.

The Shell project world

Shell invests heavily in developing new oil and gas reserves (called "green field" projects) and refurbishing existing facilities ("brown fields") to ensure the availability of the reserves it needs in order to secure its continuity as an oil and gas company. In a world where oil and gas reserves are more and more difficult to find and access, this is easier said than done, and it involves substantial investments and uncertainties. Green-field investments range from US$ 50 million to US$ 20 billion, and brown-field projects typically start at US$ 10 million. The lead times of these projects are between five and ten years from the discovery of reserves to start-up, with production periods typically lasting around 20 years. These lead times are significantly longer than the three- to four-year period that international staff members are generally expected to spend at one location. Therefore, Shell project managers seldom witness a complete project lifecycle from inception to production.

Each Shell investment program aimed at finding new oil and gas reserves follows the logic of a stage gate process (as so-called Opportunity Realization Processes, ORP). In stage gate processes, investment projects are divided into distinct stages, separated by decision "gates" (or "milestones") that must be passed before moving to the next stage of the project. At each stage gate the level of definition of the scope of projects progressively increases, reducing risk and uncertainties and hence providing clarity about the actual level of investment. Important stage gates include the concept selection and the final investment decision.

Why the Shell Project Academy was established

In 2005, Shell experienced significant delays and major cost overruns in a large part of the company's investment portfolio. This had a negative impact on production levels and the booking of reserves, but also on the reputation of Shell as a reliable business partner. The situation contributed to the reserves crisis that Shell faced when the actual progression in project milestones prevented the company from adding reserves to replace the annual production levels. In other words, the company was, proverbially, running out of gas. This was followed by intense worldwide media exposure, which triggered an equally intensive reconsideration of the company's strategy. As a result, significantly improving project delivery performance became a top priority for Shell, comparable to the importance of finding new reserves.

Shell subsequently embarked on a massive, US$ 25 billion investment program to find more reserves, targeting a minimum reserve replacement ratio of 100 percent. It resulted in the highest level of investments by private investors that has ever been seen in this industry. The investment program also included performance objectives as follows: acceleration of milestone achievement in existing projects, improved project delivery, and limitation of costs and schedule overruns to within 10 percent accuracy across the entire investment portfolio.

EXHIBIT 7.1: THE SHELL PROJECT DELIVERY PROCESS BENCHMARK

Independent, external benchmarking parties (such as Independent Project Analysis in the US) were consulted, leading to the conclusion that the Shell project and delivery processes were among the world's best. This was demonstrated by the fact that some national oil companies based their procedures on those of Shell to achieve a step change of performance in this field. Remarkably, however, some consultants asked: "Why are you not really using the project procedures yourselfs?"

Improving project delivery at Shell included three high-level objectives:

- to leverage the global presence of Shell to improve its commercial position in contracts with suppliers, contractors, and service providers,
- to improve the consistent and compliant application of Shell's project delivery processes by the upstream and downstream project delivery communities (Exhibit 7.1),
- to increase and assure the competence levels of the project delivery community.

The three objectives triggered a suite of project improvement initiatives related to governance, organization, accountability, clarity of procedures, mandates, and guidelines. The Shell Project Academy (SPA) was one of these project improvement initiatives. The Academy sought to improve staff competence levels and promote consistent compliance with company procedures under the clear vision to create a "Desired world in project land" (Exhibit 7.2). Credo: "We can no longer afford to learn solely from our own mistakes." A Shell Project Academy mission was formulated too: "To provide a world-class, accredited program to improve the competence level of project professionals capable of delivering sustained, top-quartile performance in Shell's capital investment program."

The Shell CEO at the time, Jeroen van der Veer, proactively supported the Shell Project Academy initiative in words, funds, and personal commitment, which stressed the importance of this corporate university for the company.

EXHIBIT 7.2: THE DESIRED WORLD IN PROJECT LAND

- **One pool of project managers** at all levels of competence, recognized for their professionalism and delivery performance.
- All critical roles in project teams to be assumed by internally assessed staff **within five years**.
- Staff development emphasizing individual potential, a drive to expand roles, and support of continuous competence development activities **without regard to seniority levels**.

- Habitual and **consistent application** of the company's standards, procedures, and best practices.
- Active **learning culture** embedded in the project community where information sharing and learning is truly valued and continuously sought across all activities and levels.
- Learning from recent projects and insights disseminated to the project community and embedded into the company training, standards and procedures on an **ongoing basis**.

A community-based approach

The Shell Project Academy aims to upgrade the company's capability in (complex) project management to a world-class level. To realize this aim SPA provides project management training to individuals, but also builds and sustains a project community that fulfills a vital function in the company. The development of individuals is an important building block towards the company goals, but it is not an objective in its own right.

The SPA community-based approach is based on five premises for the role of the corporate university in the organization and the scope of the program offered:

- Checks, balances, and contributions to the program should be primarily made by, for, and through the community. The SPA team should act predominantly as facilitator.
- The program should include activities focusing on cooperation and teamwork beyond the day-to-day team and across the community.
- Training courses should focus on improving consistency in the application of and compliance with project management standards, in addition to knowledge transfer across the community.
- Long-term development of individuals should reflect company talent and align with long-term community needs as well as personal interests.
- Project management is considered a form of general management in a specific environment. Hence, the SPA activities and community should connect seamlessly with the Shell Advanced Leadership Program.

Program design: Three perspectives

The nature of the SPA program for Shell can be understood best by looking at the three leading design perspectives that have been followed: content (what), target group (who), and delivery (how).

From a content perspective, the SPA program is designed to develop a set of five core project management competences, including the management of strategic and front-end processes, project execution, resources and scheduling, costs, project control, and consequences of project context. With regard to contracting and procurement, competences include the management of competitive tender processes, contract development and also contract execution. Leadership and personal skills are also part of the program. In addition to the content needs, the ORP (the Shell stage gate process to realize projects, as described above) is the central theme in all SPA courses.

From a target group perspective, one of the complexities of the SPA program design is the geographical dispersion of the target groups and the range in levels of seniority. The prime target group consists of 2,200 staff distributed over 40 countries and locations in all regions of the world, plus another 4,000 technical discipline engineers populating multidisciplinary project teams. Moreover, the project community recognizes four different levels of seniority: from project engineers, project managers, and senior project managers, to project directors. The project directors are typically responsible for multi-billion US$ expenditures per year.

From an education delivery perspective, the most important premise in the program design is that competence growth of any individual predominantly takes place in the workplace. Hence, the emphasis is placed on on-the-job training and exposure to a wide range of different circumstances. Classroom courses are seen to support and accelerate learning processes by increasing awareness of corporate goals and knowledge, creating a consistent and compliant mindset, and exploring basic skills in a safe environment.

The SPA Pentagon

The Shell Project Academy program, developed on the basis of the premises and perspectives above, is depicted in a pentagon (Figure 7.3). In tune with the

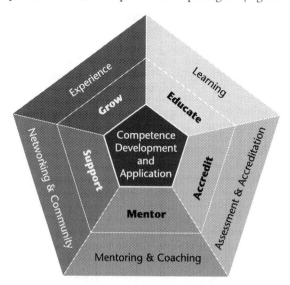

FIGURE 7.3 Image of the SPA Pentagon
Source: Adapted from Rademakers (2012)[6]

community's approach, the SPA Pentagon has become one of the widest recognized logos within the Shell organization.

As depicted by the pentagon, project management competence development – and application – are achieved through an integrated system of five complementary activities. The effectiveness of the SPA program resides in the comprehensiveness and integration of the five pentagon components. The five components are described in more detail below.

GROW refers to activities promoting competence and career development, aiming to help staff members reach the highest competence level possible in their respective careers. Key activities aim to:

- increase staff awareness of what it takes to develop personal potential,
- maximize learning from the current job through special assignments, site visits, etc.,
- increase staff awareness of development opportunities in line with ambitions.

SUPPORT refers to community building. Competence growth is stimulated when the individuals involved feel they are part of a professional community. SPA facilitates the common culture of upstream and downstream project managers building and sustaining a joint community. The single professional language and culture of the community (e.g., sharing, and daring to ask is good) helped create an effective consultation network in which to share experience and drive performance. Community building is achieved and sustained with a Project Delivery Global Network on the Internet, and Community Events (conferences) in different parts of the world focusing on regional themes and global project management issues. The community events are attended by a cross-section of regional communities and by external business parties such as contractors and consultants requested to share their perception of the Shell project community culture.

MENTOR refers to the mentoring and coaching part of the SPA pentagon. SPA offers mentoring to assist staff with career and long-term competence development, and coaching to improve daily job performance (e.g., in the fields of technology, leadership, specific knowledge). Experience shows, however, that many mentoring and coaching schemes suffer from a lack of sustainability. To counter this and improve performance, SPA has institutionalized broker sessions to bring mentors and mentees together. In addition, the effectiveness of the mentor–mentee relationship is checked on an annual basis.

ACCREDIT refers to assessment and accreditation. Annual assessments by independent parties assure and demonstrate to potential business partners that all Shell staff in critical positions on major project teams are appropriately experienced and equipped for the job. The assessments are supplemented with an assurance process by senior members of the SPA community. In addition, SPA program participants can elect to be externally accredited by an institute such as the International Project Management Association (IPMA).

EDUCATE refers to the SPA course portfolio composition, content, and delivery. While Shell has a long-lasting reputation in high-quality corporate learning programs in many technical disciplines, virtually no project management courses existed before 2005. As a consequence, Shell decided to invite a number of reputable universities and business schools[7] to assist in the development and co-facilitation of the course portfolio. This resulted in a course portfolio covering all phases of the stage gate process and catering to the learning needs of all four levels of seniority within the Shell project community (described above). The more senior the participants, the greater the emphasis on sharing experience, assuring consistency and compliance with corporate standards, and disseminating new corporate developments rather than feeding new theory. In terms of content, the portfolio includes courses covering core project management topics as well as experience areas known to be root causes of project failures in the past. The SPA portfolio delivery includes some 1,600 contact hours[8] based on blended learning approaches, promoting distance learning, and on-the-job assignments. It must be noted that while the course portfolio is comprehensive in design, only a few of the courses are mandatory. The need to attend other, non-mandatory courses depends on the nature of the knowledge gap to be filled in order to fit the specific circumstances of a particular job.

To boost effectiveness, the SPA program is deliberately linked with existing staff development processes in the wider Shell organization. For example, promotion and staff allocation processes within Shell are supported by the results of a comprehensive internal assessment that includes performance on a project management position. The project management part of the internal assessments is executed by senior leaders from the project community, who are subject to similar assessments themselves. The senior leaders will also be offered new staff based on these assessments. The approach is known to promote honesty, realism, and a greater sense of the responsibility of people working for Shell to be fair and firm.

Governance structure

The responsibility of governing the SPA activities on behalf of the Shell Executive Committee[9] is in the hands of three executive vice-presidents (EVPs): the EVP Projects Upstream, EVP Projects Downstream, and the EVP Shell Global Learning. Together they form the Academy Governance Board (Figure 7.4) chaired by the EVP Shell Global Learning, reporting directly to the Shell Executive Committee. The head of SPA reports to the Academy Governance Board.

Initiatives and propositions prepared by the team running SPA are to be approved by the Academy Governance Board. As a consequence, initiatives, changes, and developments are executed by the SPA staff under the responsibility of the three members of this board. At a first glance, observers might consider this arrangement

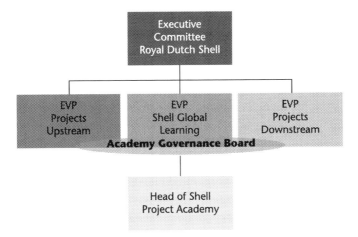

FIGURE 7.4 The Shell Project Academy governance structure

Source: Analysis by the authors

quite complicated. It is effective, though, as SPA targets are set by those accountable for managing the project communities, educational standards, and the delivery of projects. It helps to assure balanced SPA ownership. The governance structure proved to work exceptionally well, in part due to the constructive attitude of the leaders involved.

Costs and performance

The costs of initially developing the SPA program totaled over US$ 40 million. A large part of this sum went to building the course portfolio. The financial means were provided by the Shell Corporate Centre as an initial investment. After the development phase the delivery costs of the SPA program were allocated to the Shell Business Units formally employing the participants. Enforcing the benefits of a learning curve, the SPA team managed to reduce operational costs each year.

A major expenditure such as the development and operation of the SPA program calls for clarity about the return on investment (ROI). To Shell it was clear that the only clear parameter expressing the value of such an investment is the avoidance of lost Net Present Value of an investment project, due to such factors as cost overruns, delays, and loss of production. However, the analysis required to differentiate the impact of each improvement initiative was considered too time consuming, costly, and unreliable. Therefore, Shell decided against spending time and resources on trying to determine the ROI to justify SPA activities.

Shell, however, keeps close track of SPA performance. To close the loop with business requirements, leading performance indicators (Exhibit 7.3) have been formulated.

EXHIBIT 7.3: SPA PERFORMANCE INDICATORS

Main leading performance indicators

- Number of course seats taken by members of the project community against targets.
- Number of course seats taken by other technical and non-technical disciplines contributing to projects.
- Number of internally assessed staff at each level of seniority.
- Ratio of regretted/passed in the staff skill pool.
- Number of critical project positions taken by staff internally assessed by the Academy process.
- Number of mentees and mentors.
- Attendance in regional community events.
- Biannual survey of the community to assess the quality of courses; effect in the workplace; relevance of course content, material, and delivery; and sense of community.

Contributing performance indicators

- Cost and schedule overruns
- Level of severity of milestone review issues

The performance indicators are in tune with the "Desired World in Project Land" statement (Exhibit 7.2, above), which is the closest description of SPA success. Moreover, a detailed dashboard of performance indicators at the level of individuals is used for quarterly reporting to Shell management lines in HR and project communities. It allows links to be drawn between competence development and project portfolio status. It also provides a clear picture of the status of the Shell business objective to improve project delivery performance. In addition, the SPA dashboard allows internal benchmarking with other Learning & Development (L&D) organizations within Shell, and benchmarking with project management competence programs in other companies and industries.[10] The benchmarking exercises proved to be a very effective instrument to critically review cost and scope, thereby justifying budgets and activities.

SPA performance summary

The SPA team was established in January 2006. In June 2006, the first SPA learning event was launched in Kuala Lumpur. The development of the (initial scope of the) entire SPA program was completed by 2008. Since then, the SPA team has delivered approximately 1,000 seats per year representing the equivalent of 14,000 course days per year.

The number of staff with assigned mentors has grown rapidly to the desired level: all staff during their first five years in the project management community. Attendance of regional community events has increased to around 130 persons (up from 70) due to popularity. After two years and eight regional conferences, the sense of community across the two centres of excellence in upstream and downstream businesses has become stronger than ever (measured on the basis of a questionnaire). More importantly, the delivery of the project portfolio has improved significantly, even though the improvement process was interrupted by a large transformation process at Shell in 2009.

Overall, SPA is considered a success. The organization provides a major contribution to the general improvement of the project delivery function. Additionally, SPA has been instrumental in breaking down barriers that existed between the upstream and downstream project communities, which paved the way for merging these activities during the 2009 transformation.

Last but not least, external benchmarking research shows that SPA performance comes close to the much older NASA Project Academy, which is considered best-in-class.

Four critical success factors

Looking back to the process of building and developing SPA as a learning and development organization, four critical success factors can be identified:

1. *The focus of the program on the entire project community* – opposed to a focus on individuals – enables a clear connection between community performance and business objectives. The approach also allows careers and personal development to be steered towards the needs of the project community. Both effects are vital to maintaining proactive ownership among senior leaders as well as the motivation of staff to participate.
2. The comprehensiveness of the SPA program allows *integration between the program initiatives*. For example, all SPA-organized events are designed to promote the same cultural objectives. The SPA team, taking a facilitating role, ensures that activities are performed by, for, and through the community. Integration of the program with existing HR processes, such as next job allocation, is considered important too.
3. *The balanced governance structure*, proactively supported by the Shell top management, results in close cooperation between the two business lines and HR organization on policy making and the execution of competence and talent development.
4. SPA being seen as a *strong and recognizable brand* is of great importance. This has been achieved by a comprehensive change management communication strategy, including an eye-catching logo (the Pentagon), a name referring to a scientific institute (Academy), as well as extensive communication through the website, road show presentations, posters, and newsletters.

Some lessons learned in establishing the Shell Project Academy

The realization of SPA was not smooth sailing only. Below follows a selection of eight insights that have emerged along the way, which are considered to be worth sharing with other corporate universities.

1. *The advantage of senior management ownership and proactive support is not a given.* Support for a corporate university must be earned and maintained by keeping the business case top of mind. Moreover, proof must be provided that progress is being made on those parameters influenced by initiatives of corporate universities like SPA. Support is also promoted by the SPA team's willingness to demonstrate cost savings through capitalizing on the learning curve, and also making the switch from imaginative creativity during development phases to critical creativity during operations.
2. *Explain what the corporate university is NOT.* This is important to manage expectations. For example, SPA should avoid becoming the repository of project information, and it definitely is not the silver bullet to solve all problems in the project community.
3. *Be aware of short-term and long-term tension.* Tensions between short-term business targets on one hand, and long-term learning and development needs of employees on the other hand, are inevitable. Constant attention to this tension is important, as it affects the traction of the program among target groups. In the case of Shell, resolving the tension requires constantly emphasizing that large oil companies are assessed by business partners and investors on the basis of the performance of the entire portfolio, not just on individual projects.
4. *Avoid being seen as low-hanging fruit for cost cutting.* In times of economic downturn, management is easily tempted to cut costs by reducing or eliminating components of integrated programs like SPA. For instance, cutting back on the number of Community Events may seem an easy way to save money. Shell senior management has always been (made) aware of the synergy effects between the five components of the SPA Pentagon.[11] As a Shell official put it: "Don't try changing the Pentagon into a Square – it would no longer work." It would substantially reduce the overall effectiveness of the SPA program, costing more than it yields.
5. *Dare to cut back rapidly, if needed.* The SPA team started with a 40-course portfolio to be developed within 18 months, subsequently delivered to all regions of the world, and containing all major project management topics on all four levels of competence. Within a year it became apparent that the size, experience profile, and training needs of the target group did not justify this grand scale. Restructuring and cutting back to a more realistic plan proved to be necessary and was subsequently achieved.
6. *External accreditation has its limits.* The abilities of external accreditation institutes are limited and the net effect is at least questionable. For example, the test to

acquire PMI (Project Management Institute) certification is based primarily on knowledge rather than experience, performance, and behaviour. Additionally, the process to maintain the PMI accreditation could evoke unwanted effects among the workforce, such as excessive participation in PMI-recognized events just to gather accreditation points.[12]

7. *Stay clear of the ROI fallacy.* Hunting for Return on Investment evidence is extremely time consuming and only provides unreliable results. This can be seen in the light of the large number of factors affecting the Net Present Value of SPA projects, which would take many years to measure.

8. *Balance do-it-yourself and outsourcing.* Shell deliberately made use of external educational specialists to develop and deliver a program tailored to company developed processes, and based on facilitation provided by both parties.

SPA impact and challenges for the future

The Shell strategy for securing access to new oil and gas reserves in a highly competitive international environment rests on several pillars. One of these pillars is the Shell Project Academy (SPA). The corporate university was established to meet the need for excellent project delivery performance in the development of hydrocarbon reserves. The higher the performance, the better chances are of winning the competitive battle for access to new reserves.

The SPA objectives are the logical result of taking Shell business targets to the level of the project delivery community. Establishing and maintaining a clear and compelling link between business targets and the SPA program components has ensured continuous top management ownership.

SPA goes far beyond the concept of a traditional L&D organization for competence development. A major distinction is the focus on building and developing the competences of an entire (project) community in support of company objectives. The development of individuals is an important building block of the SPA activities, but not the prime objective.

The comprehensive suite of activities comprised by the SPA program is unique in scope and integration, both within and outside Shell. The synergy value created by the internal integration of the five program components,[13] and also the alignment with existing staff development and other business processes are seen as important properties. Inspired by the SPA impact, similar corporate university concepts have been adopted for the commercial and sub-surface[14] workforce of Shell.

In the international oil and gas industry SPA is widely regarded as a successful way to improve project delivery performance, which has re-enforced the Shell reputation as a reliable developer of hydrocarbon reserves. Notwithstanding this, the temptation for company leaders to sacrifice long-term goals for the benefit of short-term gains always lurks under the surface, and it is a common threat to all corporate universities. In the case of SPA, convincing Shell top management to commit to long-term investments in staff competence development is a constant challenge. Maintaining the SPA profile as one of the key drivers of competitive strength for the company will remain a challenging project in its own right.

Notes

1. This chapter describes the Shell Project Academy as it was developed and implemented from the end of 2005 until the end of 2009. Reflections on the Shell Project Academy of the past and the future, as discussed during a corporate university conference at the Erasmus University, Rotterdam, in the summer of 2012, are incorporated in this chapter.
2. IBIS World (2012), *Global Oil & Gas Exploration & Production: Market Research Report*, available at: http://www.ibisworld.com/industry/global/global-oil-gas-exploration-production.html.
3. *Financial Times* (2012), *Global 500 2012 Sector Ranks*, available at: http://www.ft.com/intl/cms/a8bbd1dc-ca80-11e1-89f8-00144feabdc0.pdf.
4. Companies' annual reports (2011).
5. BOE stands for "barrel of oil equivalent" and is an industry standard. One BOE is the approximate amount of energy released when one barrel of crude oil (about 158.9 liters) is burned. The measure of BOE helps to compare oil and gas reserves.
6. Adapted from the pentagon figure published in: Rademakers, M.F.L. (2012). *Corporate Universities: Aanjagers van de lerende organisatie*. Deventer: Kluwer. The colors used in this adapted figure differ from the source.
7. Invited universities and business schools included the University of Delft, Faculty of Technology, Policy and Management; the Queensland University of Technology, Brisbane, Australia; the Cranfield School of Management at Cranfield, England; the McCombs Business School, University of Texas at Austin.
8. 2009 figure.
9. The executive committee, at the time of establishing the Shell Project Academy, was led by Shell CEO Jeroen van der Veer.
10. Internal benchmarking is done with programs such as the extensive technical training in a number of business divisions, and also the Shell Advance Leadership program. Carrying the responsibility for external benchmarking, Human Systems (a consultancy) compares performance with the programs of 20 companies in different industries and compares the program plans and actual results by standards of the Association of Project Managers (APM).
11. This holds true for at least the time period this chapter covers.
12. This behavior is known as the "Ibansk effect" as described by the Russian writer, philosopher, and pilot Alexander Zinovjev (1922–2006). It is about the behavior of creating problems that fit the measures, instead of doing what is needed to solve problems.
13. See the section "The SPA Pentagon," featuring the components of Grow, Support, Mentor, Accredit, and Educate.
14. Predominantly the geo-scientists.

8
CANON ACADEMY: ACCELERATING TRANSFORMATION

> Learning is like rowing upstream;
> not to advance is to drop back.
> —*anonymous*

Canon Europe is active in some of the most dynamic sectors of technology-based imaging anywhere in the world. Imaging technology is not only about producing images (such as photos, documents, body scans, and microchip circuits). It is also about changing, organizing, storing, and reproducing these images (e.g., in scan, copy, transmission, and printing processes). Digitization, information technology, and in particular the smart phone and tablet computer revolution are obviously important drivers of rapid change, when we look at the way that people make use of imaging technology.

Companies in this industry must be capable of adapting quickly to rapidly changing circumstances. Global competitors of the caliber of Samsung, Sony, HP, Nikon, and ASML (and in earlier days also Kodak) are all seeking to out-innovate one another in the markets that Canon serves, including semiconductor lithography, digital cameras, lenses, medical systems, and printers. The complexity of competing in these markets rises rapidly. The value of the hardware offered, such as printers, scanners, and cameras, increasingly depends on integrated software and services. For instance, a top-quality printer will only stand a chance to sell if it comes integrated with (cloud) storage solutions, image management apps for tablet computers, and Wi-Fi. Just bolting new features and software on to imaging hardware will not work. Customers demand products to be "more smart," but also "less hard."

The demand that drives producers to integrate hardware, software, and services is accelerating. Canon "got the picture" of these changing rules of the game early on, and has adopted a vision that is elevating the company from its status as a leading imaging hardware company to the level of an integrated hardware, software, and service-driven organization in the imaging industry. The ambition of the company remains unchanged: setting the pace of development in the imaging industry.

The Canon Academy in Europe is playing an important role in transforming Canon to the shape of an integrated imaging hardware, software, and services company. Through the Academy, Canon is capable of cascading strategic vision at the corporate level into strategies that are further specified and implemented in regional and local markets. In essence, the Canon Academy takes the global corporate vision and regional mid-term plans as a point of departure and deploys organizational learning in all its facets, to use it for strategy specification, organizational development, and competence building. This chapter sheds more light on how the Canon Academy Europe, based in London, helps senior management drive strategic change through organizational learning and development.

Canon Inc. – A brief company profile

Established in 1937 in Japan and headquartered in Tokyo, Canon Inc. has always been involved in the imaging industry. By 2013 the company has become one of the world's leading players in the markets for digital cameras and printing. Canon employs more than 200,000 persons worldwide and is present on all continents. In 2012 the company recorded sales for more than 3,400 billion yen and profits exceeding 225 billion yen.

Canon Europe is organized in several business units, which include the Business Imaging Group (focused on copiers and large printers), the Consumer Imaging Group (digital cameras, lenses, camcorders, printers, scanners, broadcast equipment, and calculators), and other business units with activities covering production print, the equipment for semiconductor and LCD lithography, and medical equipment. Geographically, Canon is organized in regions (Figure 8.1), with regional headquarters in Japan, US,[1] Europe, Asia, and Oceania.

The Canon motto is *Kyosei*, which means "living and working together for the common good," and that is fundamental to the corporate mission and values. Figure 8.2 depicts the Japanese characters that stand for *Kyosei*. At Canon, there is a strong belief that contributing to the prosperity of the world and the happiness of humankind will make the company grow and develop as a corporation.

The business ambition of the company is to be the number one or two in its core markets for digital (video) cameras, video projectors, and printing, and to hold at least a number three position in all other markets where it is active. More broadly speaking, the Canon corporate goal is to become a truly global organization, joining the ranks of the world's top 100 companies. The capability to respond to dramatic change in the business environment is a key part of the long-term corporate global strategy pursued by Canon, known as the Excellent Global Corporation Plans, launched in 1996 with a series of five-year phases, of which Phase IV runs till 2015.

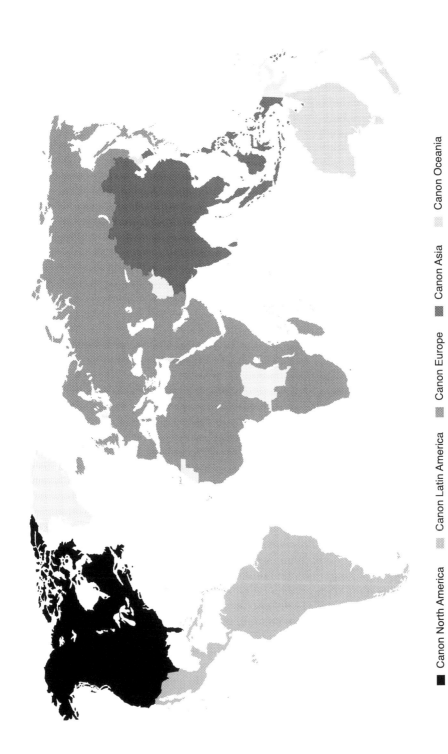

FIGURE 8.1 Canon regions

Source: Analysis by the authors

FIGURE 8.2   Kyosei in Japanese characters
Source: General font set

Strategy formation and learning at Canon

At a first glance, the strategy formation process at Canon seems quite straightforward. Top management develops the long-term plan with a time horizon of five years; senior management teams successively develop their mid-term plans with the time horizon of three years, also reviewing and adjusting these plans on an annual basis. On one hand, these plans point the company in the intended direction, also providing the necessary consistency of action throughout the vast and diverse organization that Canon is. On the other hand, the plans leave ample room for further strategy specification, which goes hand in hand with implementation. As Ronald van der Molen, director of the European Academy, puts it:

> The direction is set by senior management, but details are to be determined yet by the business. A good example is the adoption of strategic key account management for certain Canon units in Europe. It is important to understand that the concept of key account management might provide direction, but not a blueprint. The Canon units themselves must find out how to develop key account management as part of their value creation process. It boils down to learning by doing. This is the point of the strategy process where the Canon Academy comes into play.

Mid-term plans created by senior management form the point of departure for the Canon Academy. Between the mid-term plans and actual implementation lies a process of strategy specification: detailing the roles, responsibilities, organizational structures and processes, and competencies, among other necessary action. Learning is key in this process. The people involved need to find out how to make the plans work in the context of market demands and moves of competitors at the business level on one side of the picture, and organizational reality on the other. The pace of learning must be high, too. The product life cycle in the imaging industry is short: new products, services, and software are placed on the market at a very high pace. Bi-monthly cycles are no exception. As an illustration, one of the informal company wisdoms at Canon is:

> If you go on holiday for two weeks, you will miss a lot.

The transformation that Canon underwent in the market for large (professional) printers – some years ago – illustrates how the strategy formation and implementation process works. The process includes finding out what works for the company, close to the marketplace.

For decades, the Canon business for large professional printers had been focused on the "tangible technology," i.e., the hardware. Considering the long-term strategy of the company, Canon top management became convinced that they needed to offer professional printing machinery combined with service in order to sustain the company's edge over competition. Moving forward, more and more software technology had to be embedded in the printers to meet market needs – software to enable remote monitoring and servicing of the printers, for example. In tune with the long-term strategy, mid-term plans were defined at the regional level to move towards integrated printing solutions. For the European region, for instance, takeover and integration of the leading Dutch printer company Océ was part of such plans. The role of the Canon Academy came into play when organizational development questions emerged as a result of the new strategy.

The Canon Academy

In Europe, the Canon Academy acts as a team of "learning specialists" who have regular and direct contact with senior management. In addition, they are in touch with people in all the different units across the Canon organization on a daily basis. The key task of the Canon Academy learning specialists is to keep track of developments relevant to the units they serve, support strategy implementation, and to renew course curricula and programs accordingly. Managers in the organization units (known as curricula owners) implement the course curricula in collaboration with learning specialists of the Canon Academy. The curricula are a collection of specific modules for "job families." Job families are clusters of similar functions with similar knowledge needs.

The Canon Academy does not "own" the curricula, programs, or implementation processes that it helps to build. The ownership resides with top management; the Canon Academy has a supportive role and provides advice. At the end of the day it is top management that sets the direction for the organization, decides which interventions need to be made, and appoints the people who are going to work with the Canon Academy. There is a close and direct link between top management and the Canon Academy. For instance, at Canon Europe, all management teams include a member representing the Canon Academy – totaling 12 senior managers. The Canon Academy is in touch with them on a monthly or bi-monthly basis to discuss ongoing projects, new directions to take, and priorities to set. One could argue that Canon Academy provides management teams with a means of fast and direct impact on development processes in the organization. Van der Molen comments:

> It is not difficult to view the Canon Academy as an instrument for senior management to lead the organization. We have regular contact with top

management to reflect on topics concerning strategy and leadership. We reflect on, and learning from previous interventions we discuss the steps we need to take in order to keep the organization in tune with the market. In addition, we meet on a regular basis to figure out how to enable the people in the organization to actually move in the right direction, and to find out what they need to know to do so.

The Canon Academy business system

The central value proposition of the Canon Academy can be expressed as "Driving organizational change through learning" and "Helping to keep knowledge and competences up to date." Learning-driven change and development indeed form the common thread in all projects of this corporate university. Nonetheless, each project is unique and quite different in terms of time, scope, and impact. The processes and resources deployed in the Canon Academy projects are worth closer examination. The three examples below illuminate in greater detail how the corporate university helps the Canon organization to sharpen and implement new business-level strategies.

Growth in services in the printing business

A few years ago Canon felt that the company needed to adapt rapidly to a new reality in the printing business: a growing demand for solutions, i.e., combinations of products and services, instead of printing machines only. The competition for market share increasingly revolved around the capability to offer both excellent products and services to customers, attuned to specific needs. For the Canon units to move into the new direction, they had to find answers to a series of fundamental questions. What exactly is it that we are going to sell in the marketplace? What exactly are the services we are going to provide? What is the software that is – or should be – part of our new proposition? What kind of organizational structures and systems are required to make this proposition work? What are the costs?

To the people involved, it was clear that answering these questions would take solid analysis, deep product knowledge, experimentation, and access to new know-how. In other words, learning and knowledge sharing would be key for strategy implementation. The Canon Academy became directly involved, as the unit was asked to develop the new learning modules for the organization units that would implement the new strategy. Simply by asking what Canon employees needed to learn, the Canon Academy triggered many of the fundamental questions above. In the strategy interpretation, specification, and implementation processes that followed, the academy contributed by offering methods and platforms for helping to find out what the new strategy actually meant in terms of value creation, organizational development, and new capabilities.

Key account management for the consumer imaging market

Moving from a "products only" proposition towards offering solutions pushed Canon to develop new approaches to customer service. Senior management launched a plan to adopt Key Account Management (KAM) as the company's new route to the market. An important challenge for all Canon units involved, including the Canon Academy, was to find out what key account management actually meant in the context of industrial developments, market demands, and the Canon organizational heritage. This was not a quest to be taken lightly. It took several years to create the Canon way of key account management and to implement it throughout the organization.

As depicted in Figure 8.3, Canon Academy was one of the units instrumental in turning the concept of key account management into organizational reality. Early in the process, the academy took advantage of its wide network, with connections throughout the company, to form a project team. The formal aim of the team was to develop a Canon key account management learning module. The Canon Academy also deliberately added external key account management experts to the team, in order to tap their know-how. These external experts helped the project team to rapidly enhance their sales and marketing knowledge, and shared their experience about how marketing works in practice. Van der Molen comments:

> In this project it was important that the Canon Academy could take advantage of its network of external specialists who would fit well with the Canon team.

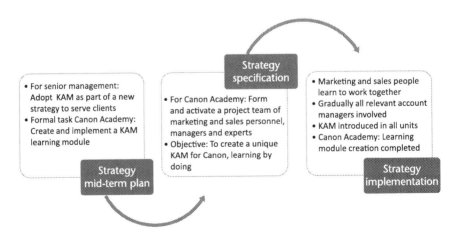

FIGURE 8.3 From strategy to implementation – adopting Key Account Management (KAM)

Source: Analysis by the author

Step by step the project team arrived at insights regarding the actual meaning of key account management for Canon, and how it should work. The sales and marketing people learned to work together more closely. It resulted in the involvement of all account managers in the new approach. Van der Molen, however, warns about a downside of the "learning by doing" approach:

> Learning by doing – aimed at finding out what works best in practice – can work well, but is not always easy. A complicating side effect is what I call the 'frustration of the pioneer': opposition against a new approach not yet accepted by all key stakeholders. Management sponsorship is of vital importance for new initiatives to stand a chance of success under such circumstances.

The impact of the project team facilitated by the Canon Academy had gradually gone beyond developing a mere learning module. In essence, the process was largely driven by questions that had to be asked, and questions that emerged along the way. Perhaps the single most impactful result achieved by the project team was the key account management model that it developed for the Canon context. Eventually, the model was used to shape key account management in all the relevant Canon units across Europe.

Launching and implementing Managed Print Service

As part of the ongoing race to out-innovate rivals, Canon developed a new proposition called Managed Print Service (MPS). MPS is a way to fully integrate all thinkable printing-related activities by combining hardware, software, information technology, and internet-based services. The capability of the Canon organization to develop new propositions of this heavy caliber, also taking them to the market rapidly, is a significant success factor. In such cases the Canon Academy helps to increase the speed to market, supporting the process from the European launch to actual implementation with a fully-fledged learning path including certification.

MPS was launched in Canon's EMEA region with a number of events, including a video message by the responsible top manager. The Canon Academy made sure this video was produced by professionals who understood the company's mentality. The objective of this video was to emphasize that the company's top management was totally committed to making MPS a success.

Next, the Canon Academy created 30-minute introductory e-learning modules about MPS and made them available throughout all units in the Canon EMEA region – in multiple languages. The module was made available through the Learning Management System (LMS, an internet-based platform). The modules, developed by the Canon Academy, introduced the essence of MPS and were followed by classroom training by product trainers. The classroom training sessions were geared to provide more detail about the MPS propositions and how they could be sold. Those who were involved in this training were expected to put what they had learned into practice, followed by a presentation-based assessment after four months.

The MPS implementation-through-learning followed a methodology Canon Academy honed over the years. Soon after the Canon top management communicated their vision of MPS as a strategic spearhead, the Canon Academy assembled a team of people from the business, trainers, and learning consultants. Aim: to build a learning module. Approach: very practical, learning along the way. Speed: high. Results: new tools and marketing strategies that formed important inputs for the e-learning modules and training being developed.

The throughput time of the massive project, including the very beginning (top management vision), exploration, building, testing, and preparing for launch was about one year. According to Van der Molen, most of the Canon Academy projects tend to take less time:

> The average throughput time of our projects is no more than six months. It is just in tune with the rapid market developments our company needs to keep up with.

Lessons learned

Over the years, Canon Academy has learned five key lessons, and three of them revolve around gaining and maintaining the senior management support without which very little can be achieved. The five essential conclusions are:

- Secure budgets large enough to enable the corporate university to have a profound impact on the organization. It is about gaining critical mass. For the Canon Academy it has been particularly fruitful to centralize the learning and development activities that were scattered across different departments and countries. Duplicate activities, processes, and initiatives were eliminated. The resultant bundling of budgets and qualities has apparently helped to achieve the critical mass which the corporate university needed to become a serious business partner for senior management.
- Corporate universities should be firmly embedded in the strategic management and leadership processes of the company. Their activities must be clearly linked to the vision and strategy of senior management. Indicators of success: senior managers begin to include corporate university results in their presentations, and they adopt models and approaches disseminated through the corporate university. To achieve "embeddedness" it is helpful to formally establish corporate university involvement in management processes, rather than leaving it to informal ad hoc processes. The formal representation of the Canon Academy in management teams, not by an academy official but by a management team member, works well for the Canon organization.

- Define clearly who is the owner of projects with corporate university involvement, and be sure it is not the corporate university. All projects should be backed by senior management.
- Avoid corporate university ownership of the programs and modules it helps to develop. Everything the corporate university does must be based on co-creation with the business, with business ownership of the resulting content, materials, and programs. Updates or renewal will be necessary at some point in time, and the business knows when – not the corporate university.
- Whatever your corporate university implements, make sure it is directly or indirectly aligned with the performance management system of the company. No alignment means little grip on the behavior of people in complex organizations managed by objectives.

Looking ahead: Canon Academy challenges

The rise of social media and pressures for empowerment pose both opportunities and threats for the way corporate universities create value. An important trend observed by Canon Academy is that individuals in organizations are increasingly becoming co-makers, rather than "takers" of knowledge and information. Companies can take advantage of this trend. In tune, the Canon Academy explores how it can play a role in facilitating and organizing user (i.e., "learner") generated content for the benefit of the Canon organization. In essence, corporate universities like Canon Academy face the challenges of balancing the benefits of decentralized and centralized approaches of learning, and avoiding the pitfalls. After all, in case of more decentralization, which is the current trend in the field of organizational learning, information overload and chaos are just around the corner.

Conclusions

Canon competes in a global industry characterized by rapidly changing markets, technologies, and strong competitors. In Europe, the Canon Academy helps the company keep up to speed with the business environment through both fast and comprehensive strategy implementation. More in particular, the corporate university is an important instrument for senior management in the processes of strategy specification and organizational development, and in capability building so that broad plans turn into concerted action by the people in the organization.

The point at which senior management usually involves the corporate university in the strategy process is when learning modules must be created as part of strategy implementation. Typically, trying to answer the question of what must be learned to enable the organization to bring the new plans into effect triggers the need for further strategy specification. At this point, the Canon Academy offers the required platforms and methods, and brings together expertise from within and outside the organization to interpret and further work out strategy through analysis, experimentation, and (rapid) learning along the way. In this process, strategy specification and implementation go hand in hand. The academy also builds the required learning modules. What the Canon Academy does not do is to "own" or manage learning modules or course curricula – managers in the business do that.

In many organizations the creation of new learning modules and curricula is seen as the last phase of strategy implementation by default. By contrast, as shown by Canon in Europe, enabling people in the organization to learn what they need to make new strategy work is the very start of an impactful strategy specification and implementation process – driven by their corporate university.

Note

1 Canon USA headquarters are based in Melville, NY; Canon Latin America headquarters are based in Miami, FL.

9
CORPORATE UNIVERSITY STRATEGY RENEWAL AT ING

Co-authors: Ruud Polet and Carin Termeer

> Nothing in progression
> can rest on its original plan.
> —Edmund Burke

Corporate universities develop and change as they adapt to shifting needs of the organizations they serve. This chapter sheds light on how the ING Business School and also its successor ING Bank Academy renew their strategy in response to fundamental changes in the organization, demonstrating the interplay between general strategy and corporate university development.

Strategic changes within the ING Group[1] form the backdrop of this chapter. Up to 2008 ING Group was one of the larger publicly listed, global bank-insurance companies in the world, employing over 100,000 people in more than 40 countries, and headquartered in Amsterdam, the Netherlands. Amidst the global financial crisis that took hold in 2008, the company required substantial loans and guarantees from the Dutch state to survive as a going concern.[2] As a consequence of this government support, the European Commission stipulated that ING Group must divide group activities to form separate banking (ING Bank) and insurance (ING Insurance) companies, and must also sell significant parts of the international banking activities. For the ING Group this has meant a disruptive shift away from a growth strategy, turning away from the ambition to be a global bank-insurance company. These recent developments have had a profound impact on the role played by the corporate university of the ING organization.

The interplay between the ING corporate strategy and corporate university activities will be described here in chronological order. The starting point is the establishment of the ING Business School (IBS) in 1998, followed by the years in which the corporate university was expanded and developed into a strategic instrument for top management – up to the financial crisis in 2008. Next, the transformation of IBS into the ING Bank Academy in the period 2009–10 is described in a context of fundamental shifts in strategic priorities.[3] The story ends in 2013, with the ING Bank Academy struggling to find a new role in a new organizational reality. At the end of this chapter, a set of lessons from the corporate university evolution process are identified and reviewed.

Building ING Business School: 1998–2002

ING Business School (IBS) was established in 1998, featuring a curriculum of company-specific courses in banking, insurance, asset management, and risk management. The initial goal of the corporate university was to teach the ING talent pool the ins and outs of the four core businesses of the company: banking, insurance, asset management, risk management. In tune, the corporate university curriculum included programs like The Art of Banking, The Art of Insurance, The Art of Asset Management, and The Art of Risk Management. These programs lasted three to four days, with cases, simulations, and instruction in English by external faculty and senior ING executives as guest speakers. As was quite in fashion in the late 1990s, the corporate university activities mainly took place in a "chateau." Over time and in line with the global presence of the company, the curriculum was offered worldwide at different ING locations.

Linking strategy and learning: 2003–8

In the course of 2003 the role of IBS in the organization began to shift from merely offering a curriculum aimed at knowledge transfer towards a vehicle with which top management could realize the international expansion strategy of the ING Group. That shift was triggered by the arrival of a new CEO, Michel Tilmant, and the new global growth strategy pursued under his leadership. The driving idea was that ING Business School "version 2.0" would enable the worldwide talent pool of approximately 4,000 persons (from early career employees to senior managers) to master the new vision, mission, strategy, goals, and values[4] of ING, and to communicate these goals to all other employees. In other words, IBS would be a key instrument to help implement the new corporate strategy.

To make the idea of strategy dissemination through learning programs work, the ING Business School portfolio of value propositions was broadened with "right-brain" issues such as leadership, management, change, engagement, culture, and diversity. For these reasons the IBS curriculum was reshaped along the lines of the Leadership Pipeline[5] concept (Charan et al., 2011), revolving around the issue of matching individual development with the requirements of certain management levels (Figure 9.1). This operation was completed in 2004.

Enlarging the scale and scope of IBS continued in the years that followed. The corporate university as an organizational unit grew in size to a team of 18 people. Most team members were program managers co-designing and administering programs run by external faculty in cooperation with senior

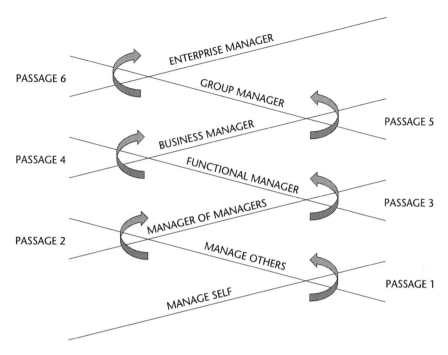

FIGURE 9.1 The Leadership Pipeline
Source: Adapted from Charan et al. (2011).

management. The number of participants started to grow rapidly from 1,000 participants initially to over 3,500 participants per year.

IBS also started to broaden the number of programs with workshops on corporate strategy subjects such as Managing for Value (a workshop on the realization of economic profit, also stressing the importance of creating shareholder value[6]). Within four years, the program was organized 200 times and over 5,000 ING employees had participated. Moreover, a High Value Specialists program was launched, aimed at specialists who perform their jobs without directly managing others. The areas in which they work vary from finance, legal, marketing, IT, and HR to other corporate functions. This group of about 1,500 employees previously had been overlooked when addressing corporate strategy execution. Between 2004 and 2008 the award-winning[7] program was held over 65 times, helping specialists to become trusted advisors to line managers in situations of strategy specification and execution. Other programs that were added to the IBS program portfolio included, for instance, Lean Six Sigma to bring the costs of services provided down and consistency up across the entire corporation.

During the years of expansion, the IBS strategy gradually shifted from a corporate-center-driven "push" approach to fill organizational learning needs towards an approach driven by division and business-unit needs. The initial "Art" programs were still "pushed" towards the corporate divisions, with mandatory

> **EXHIBIT 9.1: THE PULL APPROACH**
>
> Adopting a pro-active "pull" approach to align learning activities with organizational needs was crucial for the evolution of IBS from a traditional provider of courses towards a business partner for senior managers across the company. Key to the "pull" approach was to work with dedicated IBS account managers from every corporate division, all the while gaining in-depth knowledge of their business. It enabled a swift alignment of learning with emerging business needs. Using external experts to bring in detailed and outside-world points of view, perspectives, and examples of the business was also important. Last, but not least, to sharpen the "pull" approach, inquiries were made with other corporate universities, whereby those of General Electric, Credit Suisse, Royal Dutch Shell, and Dupont were used as sources of inspiration during the years of rapid IBS growth. The most important lesson gained during that period is that too much time or attention can never be given to the contact with corporate divisions.

participation. When creating new programs, by contrast, the director and program managers of IBS met in person with corporate division managers of ING Group to identify learning needs. As such, the corporate divisions saw their own input reflected in the programs offered, which in turn led to an increasing number of applications for the programs. Moreover, senior management commitment to act as guest speakers or coaches in the IBS programs – a key success factor – increased. One of the outcomes of the "pull" approach (see also Exhibit 9.1) followed by IBS was the International Graduate Program. The program was created in 2006 and championed by the CEO after extensive consultation of the corporate divisions. The idea was to help the divisions identify highly talented graduates who had been working at ING Group for less than a year and bind them to the organization through learning and networking. The participants would follow a program with sessions covering a host of topics and high-profile speakers across different countries, and build a cross-company personal network along the way.

Learning needs covered by IBS, whether based on "push" or "pull," always happened within the boundaries of the ING Group strategy. To make this work, regular meetings were organized between IBS and the ING Group Board of Directors, to secure a learning program alignment with the corporate mission, vision, and strategy. Moreover, quarterly ING Dialogue Series were created and facilitated by IBS. The dialogues included a member of the Board of Directors, and were based on topics raised by managers from the corporate divisions. The Dialogue Series revolved around corporate and division-level strategy alignment through questions, dialogue, and discussion, and formed an important platform upon which top management could stay in touch with the dynamics in the organization and gain first-hand feedback on the impact of their strategies.

Transition towards ING Bank Academy: 2009–11

The financial crisis of 2008 had a severe impact on the ING Group strategy. After receiving state support to survive as a going concern, the company was forced by European Union authorities to sell off substantial parts of its international business activities and also to split into separate bank and insurance companies. A new Executive Board was appointed to fulfill this task under the leadership of CEO Jan Hommen, former CFO of Royal Philips Electronics and before that Alcoa.

By 2009, the ING Group was engaged in a process of downsizing and splitting the business between the two companies henceforth called ING Bank and ING Insurance. ING Bank would continue as a publicly listed company, and the insurance part was being prepared to be sold off. The dominant motto in these years was "back to basics." Raising capital to pay back the state loans and strengthen the capital buffers of the bank had become the single top priority, rather than setting a new strategic direction for the organization in a rapidly changing business environment. Successful business units were sold, including the internet savings bank units of ING Direct in the US, Canada, and UK. Moreover, all remaining ING Group commercial and retail banking activities were tied together under a single brand and put under centralized financial control following the motto: "One bank, one balance sheet." As a result, the ING Group transformed from a world player in the bank–insurance industry into a pure play regional bank in Europe, called ING Bank.

The deep, broad, and rapid changes which the company went through, combined with the Executive Board focus on financial matters and the resulting cost containment interventions and strict travel constraints, led to a sharp decline of the attention and appetite for organizational learning and development. Despite plunging requests for existing IBS programs, however, the need for senior management to become more effective as leaders grew larger than ever under the circumstances of organizational turmoil and transformation. Many departments and business units of the newly formed ING Bank felt they needed to invest in the alignment engagement of their leaders as a way to get the organization back on track. By 2009, moreover, the need for organizational learning as an instrument for customized interventions increased sharply.

The IBS program managers and faculty adapted rapidly to the changing demand. Lead times from a first call for help to actual program delivery were reduced to less than six weeks. The corporate university had the advantage of direct access to useful content, contacts, and experience from the programs of the past. Mass customization[8] became the name of the game. Based on components of former IBS programs, for example, a customized strategy execution workshop was designed and delivered for the entire middle-management team of ING Direct France. IBS also rapidly shifted its portfolio of services towards the design and delivery of "on demand" coaching and leadership workshops. A flexible projects-driven value creation process became the new reality for IBS, instead of a curriculum-driven approach to organizational learning.

The realignment of the corporate university strategy landed well in the organization. IBS was soon reputed for good design, facilitation, and application services catering to business unit needs in turbulent times. In the meantime, however, IBS had lost its compass and mandate, which led to the end of the corporate university in its current form. An important reason for the existence of IBS had been to bring insurers and bankers together to help them better understand each other's business in order to enable the creation of synergies between both activities. With the demise of the ING Group as a bank-insurance company, this need disappeared. To make things worse, the forced split of the insurance and bank activities led to a much smaller potential audience for the IBS curriculum. Another blow confronting IBS was that with the replacement of most board members and the CEO, and the focus of the new executive board on financial survival, the corporate university lost its most important supporters. Instead of a vehicle for strategy execution or development, IBS appeared on the top management radar screen as a unit to be downsized in order to cut costs. In 2011 it was decided to merge IBS with the Commercial Banking Academy (the focused corporate university of a former ING Group division), which resulted in a new, smaller, and more focused corporate university named ING Bank Academy. IBS as a brand name had become corporate university history.

Reinventing the ING Bank Academy: 2012–13

Shortly after the corporate university merger that shaped ING Bank Academy, new challenges presented themselves to the newly established unit. The center of gravity of strategic decision making at ING Bank has shifted towards country units, i.e., business units organized geographically along national borders. In short, corporate-level decision making at the ING Bank headquarters now revolves around finance, and decision making around the alignment between markets and resources, while the realization of cross-unit synergies now resides with the country units. As a consequence, the decision making about corporate learning and the execution of learning activities have become geographically decentralized as well. The new motto is "Do local what you can do local" – including corporate learning activities. Country unit HR departments have been strengthened, focusing on people development within national boundaries. The new setting appears quite similar to the way the previously autonomous division ING Direct used to operate: mainly "local for local" and with a limited but important role for central learning and development activities to secure cross-border learning and innovation, a common culture, and access to a world class faculty network.

The recent changes in the environment of ING Bank Academy call for a next iteration of corporate university renewal. Identification and realignment with new organizational learning needs across the company will be priorities. Questions to tackle include: What could be the distinctive added value of a central corporate university located at the corporate headquarters of a geographically decentralized international bank? How to position the corporate university in a setting where central corporate functions should be small, agile, and lean? In short: what would be the new strategic compass of ING Bank Academy?

Survival or decline? 2013 as the year of truth

The year 2013 marks the beginning of the end of the final restructuring of what once was known as the ING Group. The actual split into a bank and an insurance company will take place no later than 2015, when all state loans will have been repaid, and all units to be sold will have been sold. The year 2013 also marks the arrival of the new CEO Ralph Hamers – once an IBS program participant – and more attention to long-term strategy. It is also the year to set a new focus for ING Bank Academy, though without any guarantee that 2013 will be either the year of rejuvenation or oblivion for the corporate university.

So far, ING Bank Academy has focused on serving two target groups within ING Bank: new recruits, and the top 200 managers of the company. Even in times of economic crisis the company leadership considers it very important to be able to compete for talented university graduates. An attractive young talent program is one of the key instruments to attract the graduates that ING Bank wants to bind to the company in order to secure the continuity of succession plans for key positions. For the ING Bank target group of graduates the term "attractive" is synonymous with "a global program" and opportunities for (short) assignments abroad. The need is seen for a corporate-level unit to build, design, and maintain such a global trainee program – and above all to avoid reinventing the wheel. The same is true for the top 200 programs. More than ever before, bank executives need to be deeply knowledgeable of the banking system, but they also need the capability to create followership in order to execute new strategies. In tune, ING Bank Academy has been made responsible for the design, and implementation of a Senior Bankers Program. Another lifeline for ING Bank Academy survival is the need for solid and well-developed banking skills, as the banking industry incumbents have realized what forces actually caused the financial crisis to happen. Accordingly, observers have begun to wonder if the former IBS Art of Banking series might gain relevance again – though in a form fitted to the decentralized nature of ING Bank.

The jury is still out regarding the survival or decline of ING Bank Academy. Although there are reasons to believe that ING Bank Academy will start a new corporate university life cycle and grow along with a rejuvenating ING Bank, indicators for a dim future are also present. It is by no means sure that ING Bank Academy will survive the implications of a new and upcoming investigation about the role and importance of all staff functions and corporate departments of the bank. ING Bank faces the challenge of committing to a cost-to-income ratio[9] of 55 percent in 2015, meaning that cost cutting will increase again, as income levels will be hard to raise under circumstances of depressed markets and tighter international regulations. Only later in 2013 will ING Bank Academy know if it has a future.

Lessons learned and conclusions

In the span of 15 years, ING Business School has gone through a life cycle of startup, growth, maturity, and decline, and, perhaps, rejuvenation (Figure 9.2).

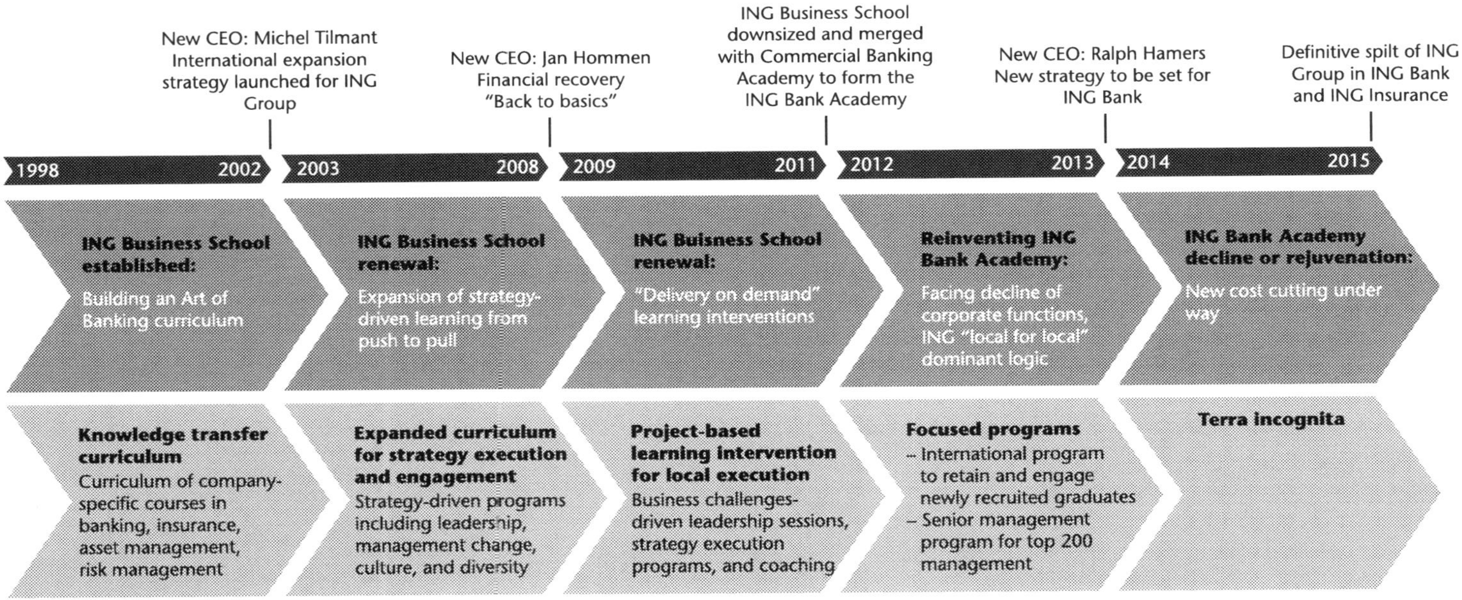

Timeline (top labels)

- **1998**
- **2002–2003**: New CEO: Michel Tilmant. International expansion strategy launched for ING Group
- **2008–2009**: New CEO: Jan Hommen. Financial recovery "Back to basics"
- **2011–2012**: ING Business School downsized and merged with Commercial Banking Academy to form the ING Bank Academy
- **2013–2014**: New CEO: Ralph Hamers. New strategy to be set for ING Bank
- **2015**: Definitive split of ING Group in ING Bank and ING Insurance

Middle row (ING Business School phases)

- **ING Business School established:** Building an Art of Banking curriculum
- **ING Business School renewal:** Expansion of strategy-driven learning from push to pull
- **ING Business School renewal:** "Delivery on demand" learning interventions
- **Reinventing ING Bank Academy:** Facing decline of corporate functions, ING "local for local" dominant logic
- **ING Bank Academy decline or rejuvenation:** New cost cutting under way

Bottom row (curriculum/programs)

- **Knowledge transfer curriculum:** Curriculum of company-specific courses in banking, insurance, asset management, risk management
- **Expanded curriculum for strategy execution and engagement:** Strategy-driven programs including leadership, management change, culture, and diversity
- **Project-based learning intervention for local execution:** Business challenges-driven leadership sessions, strategy execution programs, and coaching
- **Focused programs:**
  – International program to retain and engage newly recruited graduates
  – Senior management program for top 200 management
- **Terra incognita**

FIGURE 9.2 ING Business School evolution

Source: Analysis by the authors

Having offered a curriculum of courses in the early years, moving towards a strategic role and being institutionalized as a vehicle of corporate strategy implementation marked the steps towards maturity. Decline set in with the metamorphosis into the smaller and lower profile ING Bank Academy, losing critical mass.

The way ING Business School transformed into the ING Bank Academy shows how the priority and role of corporate learning in organizations can change quite dramatically in a short timeframe. Even under harsh circumstances and turbulence, however, the need for organizational learning remains, but with different characteristics than in times of relative stability. Organizational learning needs shift away from courses and towards projects, from management to leadership capabilities, and, in the case of ING Bank, also from a global to a local-for-local approach.

At least two messages can be derived from the experience of running a corporate university at a bank both in times of growth, and in more than five years of turmoil in international banking. The message to senior management is to take advantage of their corporate university in executing a strategy – by enabling people in the organization to do just that. Reversely, corporate university programs enable top management to hear, on the basis of first-hand inputs, what is going on in the organization. For corporate university leaders it is essential to realize the crucial importance of having a sponsor on the Board, a clear mandate, and a tight value creation focus. Moreover, in times of aggressive cost cutting, the reduction of corporate university activities to value creation for a small set of target groups pivotal to the company promotes the chances to survive.

If one thing has become clear to ING Business School and its successor ING Bank Academy, it is that corporate university renewal in times of growth is a matter of ambition and the attitude required to excel. By contrast, in times of sharp organizational decline, companies may be tempted to throw the baby out with the bath water – cutting costs but also cutting the capability to adapt to changing circumstances. Under such circumstances, corporate universities need to be more agile and have a sharper strategic profile than ever before.

Notes

1 ING stands for Internationale Nederlanden Groep, which is the result of a merger between the insurance and bank companies Internationale-Nederlanden and NMB Postbank Groep. ING was the first financial organization in the world to have banking, insurance and asset management under one roof.
2 The bank was considered a "system bank", i.e., part of an international financial infrastructure to be saved from collapse through state support.
3 Corporate learning at ING Insurance has also engaged in a process of fundamental renewal. The corporate university of ING Insurance is called NN Academy (NN stands for the brand name Nationale Nederlanden). In contrast to the ING Bank Academy, the NN Academy did not evolve from the ING Business School, but from the ten-year-old Bank Insurance Academy that was part of the insurance division of ING Group. The NN Academy will not be covered in this chapter revolving around the evolution of ING Business School and its successors.

4 An example of a direct intervention by Tilmant is the 2006 conference in Berlin with the top 200 managers of the ING Group. All managers found a book on the pillow of their hotel bed, which had the title *Why Should Anyone Be Led By You?* (Goffee and Jones, 2006). Tilmant demanded of the managers that they read the book, reflect on it, and put the principles (boiling down to authentic and skillful leadership) into practice.
5 One could argue that the concept resembles a management slalom rather than a leadership pipeline. Notwithstanding this, the principle of managers facing different requirements at different levels when leading people has proven helpful for companies worldwide to shape their management development programs.
6 These were widely accepted topics at that time.
7 The program (labeled as a High Impact Performance program) received the EFMD Excellence in Practice Award.
8 The concept of mass customization boils down to building unique products and services on the basis of standardized building blocks, just like many different objects can be created with Lego bricks.
9 The ratio is also known as C/I ratio and calculated by dividing a company's operating costs by its operating income.

Literature

Charan, R., S. Drotter, and J. Noel (2011). *The Leadership Pipeline: How to Build the Leadership Powered Company.* 2nd edition. San Francisco: Jossey-Bass.

Goffee, R. and G. Jones (2006). *Why Should Anyone Be Led By You? What it Takes to be an Authentic Leader.* Boston: Harvard Business School Press.

10

BRINGING SPEED TO KNOWLEDGE: A DEAN'S JOURNEY

> It is good to have an end to journey toward,
> but it is the journey that matters in the end.
> —Ursula K. Le Guin

The world of lighting is changing rapidly. For companies in the lighting industry, the rules of the game are changing as a result of the rise of LED technology, which is revolutionizing the business and making the once-dominant sources of light, such as light bulbs and fluorescent lamps, obsolete. That is the context in which Philips Lighting University fulfills its role, ensuring that the people of Philips Lighting acquire and build the knowledge and expertise they need to keep their company abreast of the competition. A world market leader in lighting products and services, Philips Lighting is headquartered in the Netherlands.[1] The company competes, among others, with the lighting divisions of technology giants such as General Electric (US) and Siemens (Germany).

The Philips Lighting University serves thousands of people worldwide in a consistent and transparent way. As part of Marketing, and not HR, it makes use of a certification system to create demand for corporate university services, also covering customer learning, and running a popular website on the corporate intranet. The Philips Lighting University approach to organizational learning is innovative, and it stands out in a world where the majority of organizations struggle to create "pull" (employees demanding corporate university services) and to scale up learning services, where "learning" is seen more often than not as a function belonging to Human Resource Development (HRD) rather than Marketing.

The way this corporate university works can largely be traced to a long, step-by-step process of pioneering, development, and learning along the way. More in particular, key components of the corporate university strategy are rooted in the 16 years of learning at six organizations in four different countries experienced by the founding dean of the Philips Lighting University, the native Belgian Stefaan van Hooydonk. This chapter is shaped along the lines of his international journey, starting halfway through the 1990s in China in a rapidly growing business school (CEIBS), continuing at Nokia (telecom industry) in China and later in Finland, then moving on to Vlerick (a business school) and Agfa HealthCare (an imaging company focused on healthcare) in Belgium, and finally arriving at Philips Lighting. Along this career path he has developed corporate university-relevant practices and capabilities including the operation of a corporate university as a business. He has been the driver of strategic renewal, he has pioneered new ways to reach economies of scale and scope, and he has increased the impact of organizational learning by getting people to "want to learn" instead of "having to learn". The last sections of this chapter describe how these elements are integrated within Philips Lighting University and how they have brought about a paradigm shift in organizational learning, in the end living up to a strategic imperative to bring speed to knowledge.

Going East: Pioneering in China

The journey of the dean starts in 1994 in China, with a position as executive education director at the China Europe International Business School (CEIBS) based in Shanghai. His major activity at CEIBS is to establish and lead an executive education unit for a business school funded by the European Union. The unit grows rapidly into an organization with a headcount of 25 people and a turnover of US$ 7 million within five years. The corporate university-relevant experience he collects here includes the fundamental processes of pioneering, building, and leading an educational organization in an international setting, and teaching there.

The CEIBS success does not go unnoticed, and in 1998 Van Hooydonk moves to Beijing at the request of Nokia, a mobile telephone and networks manufacturer from Finland, to help grow the company in Greater China from 3,000 to 8,000 employees in the course of three years. The Nokia corporate university in China becomes a growth machine, providing knowledge transfer in a range of both non-technical and technical areas. The sheer number of people to be trained on the basis of similar content poses a problem, as well as the fact that Nokia is operating at more than 20 different sites across China. Learning has to be scalable (i.e., scaled up both geographically and in terms of volume) as it is not possible to have thousands of people trained on time and at reasonable costs, if they all have to travel to the corporate university premises in Beijing.

Ways to bring learning to the masses have to be found, and e-learning (at the time in an infant stage of development) appears on the radar screen. Hence, the corporate university of Nokia in China launches an e-learning application based on dial-in network technology with a mere bandwidth of 21 kbit/s (compare this with the 200 kbit/s of 3G mobile technology). Needless to say, this means that the newly hired Nokia employees in China have to be patient during the act of accessing what the corporate university has for them. Finding a way to motivate these learners to endure the early-stage application of e-learning is obviously essential to the success of the corporate university. The solution found here is to combine e-learning with certification (derived from an established Cisco[2] certification system), to link learning achievements with status. As an effect, people even begin to invest their spare time in learning, aiming to obtain status-enhancing certificates[3] more rapidly.

Moreover, they build an initial learning management system (LMS) to manage and support efficient learning at Nokia locations across the country. Essentially, the system helps to keep track of the number of employees at the company who earn a certification. Apart from pioneering and developing e-learning in China for Nokia, the corporate university also engages in the design and delivery of management education, including classroom sessions, coaching, and follow-up.

Moving North: Global e-learning from Finland

In 2001 Nokia management asks Van Hooydonk to become the global e-learning director at their headquarters in Finland. Responsibilities include starting up, giving strategic direction to, and integrating e-learning for the company on a global scale. In this e-learning position Van Hooydonk reports to global HR (human resources), but the reporting line soon changes to global e-business. The driving idea is that thinking has to move away from the classical setup of learning in classrooms towards a learning concept that allows for scaling up at marginal costs. This must be seen in the context of Nokia experiencing rapid growth in the worldwide market for mobile telephones and network equipment. Van Hooydonk recalls:

> It was time to think different, and to think big.

Thinking big is an absolute necessity in the light of the ambition not only to train Nokia employees worldwide with e-learning applications, but also to include business partner and end-user training. In the case of Nokia, this means reaching out to over 200 million online learners. Moreover, to seduce end users to learn how to get the most out of their Nokia products, learning has to be made easily accessible and fun. Pioneering mobile learning and "edu-gaming" (games with the aim to educate) becomes the name of the game at Nokia headquarters.

One of the programs that has to be developed – in 13 different languages – is aimed at business partners: the shops that sell Nokia handsets, scattered across the world. New telephone models are being introduced at a high pace – consumers buy a new handset at intervals of 12 to 18 months. The challenge for Nokia is to ensure that the next handheld device is one of theirs again. It is essential to keep the shops up to speed with the high pace of new handheld releases, and this may be where the concept "bring speed to learning" first emerges. Webinars would come in handy – but they do not exist yet. For a rapid transfer of knowledge about new telephone models to large numbers of people, Van Hooydonk and his team have to pioneer their own solutions. One solution is the creation of 30-minute video clips – but this does not work. The sales people it is intended for refuse to watch longer than three minutes or they refuse to watch the videos at all. Interestingly, Nokia also produces a series of short videos lasting two to three minutes to instruct Nokia repair shops (also scattered around the world) on ways to repair the latest telephones. Van Hooydonk realizes:

> You can learn a lot in just two minutes.

Accordingly, the department replaces their 30-minute videos with very short ones no longer than three minutes in duration, enticing sales people to watch them and learn.

The need to find a way to make learning not only fun, but also relevant and user-friendly provides important insights in the challenging development of learning solutions capable of reaching very large numbers of learners at the same time. For the same reason, they take initial, exploring steps in the field of edu-games to teach consumers smart ways to use their mobile phones. In addition, they launch a "how-to site" (FAQ based) for consumers – promoting self-education.[4] That helps Nokia bring down costs, as the application replaces calls to the Nokia call center, where the company has been paying €10 per call. After a little more than two years, the pioneering job comes to an end for Van Hooydonk in Helsinki, as the notoriously long, dark, and cold winters of Finland begin to take a toll.

Back to the Southwest: A sort of homecoming in Belgium

The next step in the dean's journey is a homecoming for Van Hooydonk in two respects: returning to Belgium and joining a business school again in 2004. His position as senior manager of executive education at Vlerick Management School is a stepping stone toward another pioneering role in corporate learning, as the head of Agfa Academy, the corporate learning arm of Agfa HealthCare[5] based in Mortsel, Belgium. The initial assignment is to modernize the Agfa Academy *the Nokia way*, reporting directly to the company's chief marketing officer (CMO). Here again, investments in the corporate university are driven by the strategic importance of the need to integrate newly acquired businesses more rapidly and successfully through learning-based change management interventions.

Modernizing the Agfa Academy extends well beyond *the Nokia way*, first because Agfa is totally different from the mobile telephony giant – though also a global, technology-driven company. Second, e-learning embarks on a second wave of development in 2005. With the emergence of the new e-learning authoring tools (comparable with the possibility to build one's own website) e-learning needs can be met by the corporate university itself, instead of engaging external vendors. This reduces the solution development time from 12 weeks to 12 hours – along with better control over the contents. Innovations like webinars and virtual classrooms are introduced as well – though it remains difficult to get potential corporate university students to actually use these tools.

Along with the enhancement of e-learning and construction of a supportive Learning Management System, two new components are added to the corporate university repertoire. First, the learning programs are now certified, strengthening the perceived value of these learning modules. Second, the Agfa Academy starts reaching out to important partners outside the organization, being the dealers of Agfa products. The philosophy is simple: making Agfa dealers more effective makes Agfa HealthCare more effective, too. Based on the same philosophy, the corporate university starts to develop customer training, including the "eye candy" (i.e., attractive "looks" of e-learning environments) to help entice customers – such as medical doctors – to make use of the Agfa Academy e-learning applications and pay for it.

Last but not least, Agfa Academy engages in a paradigm shift under the leadership of Van Hooydonk. Instead of offering a curriculum of periodically updated programs and courses, the corporate university strategy is now to become the ultimate source of "continuous reference material" for the company and its stakeholders. The driving idea is to generate "pull" by offering the latest knowledge, information, and learning solutions ranging from product updates to certifications for trade shows. As a result, more than 60 percent of the Agfa Academy users return to its website to access the latest information and learning offer on a monthly basis. Van Hooydonk about the "content pull" approach for Agfa Academy:

> To make this work, we had to move away from thinking in terms of top-down management and centralization, and understand the benefits of decentralized content creation driven by empowerment, knowledge sharing, transparency, and clear communication. It worked. Instead of being a unit from headquarters, the Agfa Academy more and more became seen as *our* academy, helping to do our jobs and perform our tasks successfully.

For Agfa Academy more in particular, to move towards more decentralization is to rebalance the global standardization of learning content and approaches on one hand against local adaptation on the other hand. The synthesis between these two opposite approaches is, in essence, based on a highly standardized e-learning infrastructure which enables the dissemination of user-generated content. This infrastructure benefits from the large, global scale of the Agfa Academy, which allows for substantial investments in state-of-the-art software, equipment, design, and programming and at the same time leverages the value of the academy's user-generated content. Instead of getting stuck in the ongoing centralization-or-decentralization debate and sub-optimal compromises between the two approaches, a new balance is created, combining the strengths of both.

For Van Hooydonk, pioneering, modernizing, and also commercializing Agfa Academy comes to an end by 2010, as the reporting lines of the corporate university are changed – there is a shift away from the Board and towards the Human Resources department. It is time to move on and add a new chapter to the journey of the dean. New challenges wait around the corner, just about 56 miles away in Eindhoven, Netherlands, at Philips Lighting.

Moving on: Creating the Philips Lighting University

In 2010 the CEO of Philips Lighting, Rudy Provoost, asks Van Hooydonk to develop a corporate university that can help tackle an important strategic challenge facing the company and its distributors. LED technology has begun to revolutionize the entire industry on a global scale, with new business systems replacing the ones that have been around for more than a hundred years. Van Hooydonk comments:

> The impact of LED technology is comparable with the introduction of the electrical powered candescent lamp in the 19th century, replacing gas and oil lamps and candles as the major sources of light, and triggering the emergence of new business models.

The underlying force of this new industry-wide revolutionary change is the fact that LEDs are silicon-based electronic components, just like transistors and microchips.[6] In tune, the speed of innovation in LED is much higher than ever seen in incandescent (the light bulb) and fluorescent (tube light, and compact fluorescent light or CFL) technology.[7] As Van Hooydonk explains:

> The life cycle of an LED-based product is about 6 to 9 months – this is the time it takes before a newer version enters the market. For light bulbs the product life cycle is about 12 years, and for CFLs roughly 9 years.

It is not difficult to see that this has a profound influence on how sourcing, production, services, marketing, and distribution are shaped and organized. As an industry observer points out:

> The life cycle of an LED-based product might be 6 to 9 months, but the life time of the product is up to 50,000 hours, compared to approximately 1,000 for a light bulb and 8,000 for CFLs. The LED proposition is different and replacement sales are different – if any replacement of the same LED-based light source happens at all.[8]

In the vision of the Philips Lighting leadership, outperforming the competition in the new era of LED technology not only requires faster product innovation, but also much faster organizational learning to make sense of the revolutionary changes confronting the company, distributors, installation companies, and also industrial users and consumers. In short, learning has come to be a key competitive component of a thriving business in times of industry-level system change. The assignment given by top management to Van Hooydonk: "Bring speed to knowledge" on a global scale. To secure an outward perspective and a commercial mind-set, the corporate university is positioned within the office of the CMO.

As dean of the Philips Lighting University to be created, Van Hooydonk decides already at the start in 2010 that they must cover the learning needs of their employees *and* customers alike. This requires a change of the traditional paradigm of organizational learning. Instead of thinking in terms of curricula, courses, and classrooms within the borders of an organization, thinking should be in terms of bringing more speed to knowledge across the entire industry ecosystem. As Van Hooydonk calls it:

> A joined-up, business-aligned and course-independent way of taking organizational learning online via a range of delivery devices.

To put this strategic vision for the corporate university into practice, Van Hooydonk and his team place their focus on five shaping principles:

- Create "pull." People should be enticed to learn, instead of being pushed.
- Provide certification. Bring transparency to the mastering of knowledge.
- Measure the effects of learning in simple and sensible ways (number of visits to Philips Lighting University websites, number of certificates).
- Digitize content via multiple methods including webinars, e-books, self-study e-learning packages, mobile learning, product wikis, games, and videos.
- Incorporate informal learning and performance support in the learning mix.

The capability to *entice* large numbers of people to learn – all 54,000 of those working for Philips Lighting across the globe, plus those working for distribution partners, and later on also customers – is the very essence of Philips Lighting University. A setting has been created in which large numbers of people feel the need to learn about topics relevant to the strategy of the organization. In this setting, the corporate university seeks to empower its "students" instead of trying to manage them. The approach hinges on a certification system that helps to evoke organization-relevant learning needs. At a first glance, the certification system seems rather simple – as depicted in Figure 10.1 – but the system works more subtly and powerfully than one might expect.

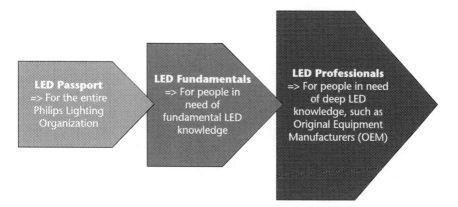

FIGURE 10.1   Philips Lighting levels of certification

Source: Adapted from Philips Lighting University documents

Earning a certificate comes with the right to carry specific Philips Lighting titles, which appears to work as a source of social status. The elegance of the certification system is that it not only helps to motivate people to learn in a particular direction, but also helps the corporate university to measure results (i.e., how many people of which unit in which country have earned a certificate) and make the results transparent. As an effect of the pull approach – focusing on learning outputs instead of inputs – and the transparency reached through the measurements – Philips Lighting University has done away with the learning management system (LMS).

Though the pull-generating certification system is an innovation customized to the firm (in this case Philips Lighting), it is not an innovation new to the world. For instance, an organization like Cisco (a US-based global firm providing internet equipment and services) has been taking advantage of the motivational effects of certification for more than a decade. Similarly, Starbucks makes use of the mechanism of social status (*baristas* with a black instead of a green apron are in higher esteem) motivating people to acquire company-relevant knowledge and skills, and developing them into coffee experts.[9] The experience of the Philips Lighting University dean years ago, with certification at Nokia in China, is likely to have sparked the idea of certification to mobilize large numbers of people and engage them in organizational learning. Exhibit 10.1 describes the Philips Lighting certification system in more detail.

For the "pull" approach to organization learning to succeed, providing the right inputs is essential. But what are the right inputs? At Philips Lighting University, a broad, attractive, and easily accessible offer of learning opportunities is considered to be prerequisite. To make learning fun is another important ingredient. Hence, virtually the whole spectrum of internet-based learning is deployed. The leading principle is that people start looking for knowledge and information fit for their needs.

The logic behind the way the Philips Lighting University learning propositions are structured is that training, certification, and performance support are all part of a single continuum. The continuum covers the learning needs of people with different levels of experience in LED technology. As depicted in Figure 10.2, new employees (but also customers and even consumers) are helped to *get* up to speed, while experienced people are supported to *keep* up to speed and stay current. Getting up to speed happens with training "push," keeping up to speed is "pull" based.

Philips Lighting University has not been built all at once, but in a number of steps – quick steps, though. The rollout of the "backbone" programs consisted of three waves and took three years. Each wave has involved more and more people within or associated with Philips Lighting. The first wave, starting in 2011, aimed at sales and marketing people, plus new hires. Over 2,000 people earned an "LED passport" certificate by the end of February; and in August there were more than 10,000 owners of the certificate. The organization-wide rollout aimed at the business-to-business domains of Philips Lighting followed in 2012. The third wave, also organization-wide, included the business-to-consumer business. Moreover, the corporate university offer has been broadened with programs for newly recruited

EXHIBIT 10.1: CREATING "PULL" AND OUTPUT CONTROL THROUGH CERTIFICATION

A certificate in the conventional sense of the word is often not much more (and nothing less) than a proof of competence. In the Philips Lighting University context it is much more than just that. The certificate has been cultivated as a source of pride, motivation, and confidence for employees. For their managers the certification system brings transparency about the knowledge levels of the people they lead and helps to identify the (rising) stars. Moreover, it helps them to work with measurable standards. Beyond the borders of Philips Lighting – more in particular, on the part of Philips Lighting customers – the certification system inspires confidence in working with the people from their partner and/or supplier of LED-based products and services.

The creation of the certification system started when the corporate university brought LED technology and business experts together. Together they have built a set of more than 500 questions and answers that cover LED-related knowledge which people in and around the organization should have to make them successful in their work – and, by doing so, making Philips Lighting more successful than the competition.

The set of questions form the basis for tests with different levels of advancement, and different levels of certification. The tests are challenging (and increase in complexity when moving to the next test) so people feel proud when passing. The difficulty of the test, the social effects of people sharing the fact that they passed (or not), and the certificate and title attached to it, have been instrumental in making the test go viral throughout the organization. People want to get the certificates. In this way, the certificated are valued and become a driver of self-managed learning in an environment with multiple sources of knowledge offered by Philips Lighting University. The number of sources used and time needed to learn enough to pass the tests differ from person to person. Those who do not pass the test receive more support from Philips Lighting University with e-books, wikis, e-learning, and edu-games among other possibilities.

Measuring learning progress and making it transparent helps to keep track of both individual development and the impact achieved by Philips Lighting University on an organization-wide level. In terms of impact, an indicator is the number of visits to the Philips Lighting University website (giving access to a range of learning opportunities), making it the seventh most popular Philips site worldwide, with an average page view time of no less than 14 minutes.

New employment →	Organizational learning →	Seasoned employee
Training: "Getting up to speed" + mainly formal + one-to-many + push + separate activity	**Certification:** "Proof of knowledge" + LED Passport + LED Fundamentals + LED Professionals	**Performance support:** "Staying current" + mainly formal + many-to-many + pull + part of daily work

FIGURE 10.2 Getting and keeping knowledge up to speed

Source: Philips Lighting University documents

employees ("Connected2Lighting"), a consumer learning portal, B2B customer training, performance support tooling, programs for internal and external business understanding (trends, competitive insights, etc.), all on a global scale.

In the first three years of its existence, Philips Lighting University has become a driving force behind high-volume organizational learning through a mechanism which evokes company-relevant learning needs in a deliberately targeted audience ("pull"). People within and around the organization are enabled to learn the way they prefer most, having access to a broad range of internet-based self-study propositions ranging from short videos and e-books to games and webinars. Results are measured and made transparent in the number of certificates awarded. It is safe to say that the assignment to bring speed to knowledge has been mastered successfully. It would be too soon to say, however, that Philips Lighting University has little left to pioneer, explore, and develop.

The next challenge that Van Hooydonk and his team take up is to strike a new and impactful balance between formal learning based on explicit, codified knowledge on the one hand, and informal learning based on tacit, implicit knowledge on the other. Both are important but, so far, the corporate university has mainly focused on formal learning. However, it is seen to be at least as important for the organization to speed up, enhance performance, and innovate the mechanisms of tapping tacit knowledge.[10] Hence, most – if not all – of the 2013 Philips Lighting University research budget is directed towards making informal learning work for the organization – experimenting with internet-based technology to eliminate barriers such as geographical distance. Here, the key challenge is: How can we make it easy for people in the organization to get together and learn from each other – preferably just as easily as it is currently to access formal knowledge *on demand*? Van Hooydonk says:

> There are not many industry best practices on informal learning on a global scale yet. It feels like we are opening Pandora's Box – in a positive sense.

The corporate university pays much attention to unlocking the potential of learning communities, team learning based on connecting people located in different parts of the world through video-supported workshops, and also to the development of modern versions of master–apprentice schemes.

Informal learning and performance support have begun to converge in services explored by Philips Lighting University which are aimed at helping sales people be more productive. The key question is: Where do our sales people seem to lose time when doing their jobs? Van Hooydonk answers:

> We have analyzed how much time sales people tend to spend searching knowledge and information when developing a client proposal. The time spent is about three to five hours per week. Our ambition is to help bring this number down by ten to fifteen percent through performance support.

Research by Philips Lighting University has revealed that an important part of the knowledge sales people search for appears to be implicit in nature: it is present in the heads of their colleagues. Hence, the corporate university has commenced pioneering and testing ways to access the tacit knowledge of Philips Lighting sales people around the world on a "just in time" basis. A promising example is the creation of "flash communities" of sales people across different geographical regions. By 2014, the community members will use video-supported learning approaches to instantly share experiences and practices when they are in the process of creating client proposals. Marketing campaigns deployed to draw attention to this kind of learning opportunities show that it is an effective way to create demand. True to its nature, Philips Lighting University works along the lines of a pull-based, scalable, and technology-driven approach again – a formula that also appears to work well for informal learning.

Insights worth sharing

From the very start of the dean's journey, a key insight that emerged is that corporate universities benefit from being run like a business. Keywords are: transparency (about results), pull (need-driven), and strategic positioning (distinctiveness). A business mind-set will also be helpful to bring speed to knowledge – i.e., faster and better access to knowledge, information, and learning. Such speed is important for more and more organizations that need to stay aligned with a rapidly changing environment. Speedy access to knowledge also benefits from a heavy use of digital technology, enabling the speed-up and scale-up of learning through mobile devices, self-study e-learning facilities, communities, games, videos, and more. It is important to realize that technology should stay in the background. It is the user experience that counts.

Another insight worth sharing is that advances in digital technology have unlocked the possibility for individuals to take responsibility for their own learning in organizations. To make this work, people in organizations not only need to be provided with flexible access to a range of learning resources, but they also have to be motivated to learn what is relevant to the organization. In other words, with the individual ownership of learning, it takes more effort than before to secure the alignment of individual and organizational interests. Aligned with the ongoing individualization of learning, moreover, it is more efficient to take proof of knowledge as the starting point and follow up with knowledge acquisition – not the other way around. Last but not least, organizations can benefit substantially from the often untapped potential of decentralized content creation through wikis and other digital platforms.

Conclusions

The *journey of the dean* through time and space has yielded a range of effective corporate university arrangements for organizations pursuing growth and innovation strategies. The companies involved have witnessed corporate universities as growth machines (Nokia), change machines (Agfa HealthCare), and, more and more, as a vehicle of strategic renewal (Philips Lighting). As depicted in Figure 10.3, the corporate university arrangements created during "the journey of the dean" comprise a broad range of different practices and value propositions: reaching thousands (and later millions) of learners inside and outside company borders, up-to-date user-generated reference materials, certification systems, and speeding up organizational learning, to name a few.

Notwithstanding the width and depth of the repertoire built by our dean when crossing borders, industries, and companies, a common thread is discernible. All corporate university "stations" share a clear and direct link with strategy, embracing state-of-the-art technology, being transparent about results, and moving away from the management of organizational learning to the empowerment of people to learn.

The successes harvested so far do not mean that the dean's journey is likely to come to an end soon. Three major and ongoing balancing acts face our dean – and many corporate university leaders – which call for ongoing exploration in the field of corporate learning:

1. How to balance decentralization and centralization of content creation to achieve the right scope of knowledge the organization needs to be able to access?
2. How to balance control and empowerment to align individual learning with organizational needs?
3. How to balance formal and informal learning to make learning in the organization as effective as possible?

New answers to these balancing acts are likely to unlock innovative ways for corporate universities to bring speed to knowledge. Reasons enough for the dean's journey to continue – preferably at full speed.

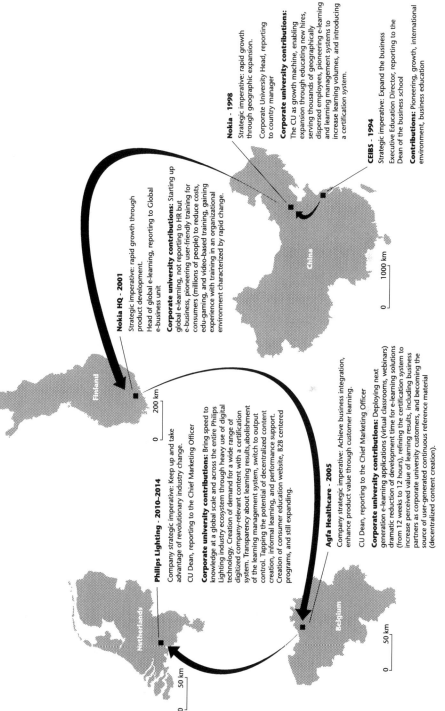

FIGURE 10.3 Overview of a dean's journey, 1998–2014

Notes

1. Philips Lighting is a division of Royal Philips Electronics NV, a publicly listed company headquartered in Amsterdam, the Netherlands, which also includes a Health division (medical equipment and technology-based services) and a division for Domestic Appliances (ranging from coffeemakers and shavers to water purifiers).
2. Cisco, an American company, is among the largest global players in routers, switches, and other internet equipment and services.
3. The effect is also known as WIIFM ("What's in it for me?"). In this case, the "what" is social status.
4. Name of the site: www.nokiahowto.com.
5. Agfa HealthCare, a division of the Agfa-Gevaert Group, is an international supplier of diagnostic imaging, contrast media, and IT services for hospitals and other healthcare organizations.
6. The difference means that LEDs consume much less energy to generate light than candescent and fluorescent sources of light.
7. The high pace of innovation is driven by the LED technology itself (more light per watt, colors, etc.) but also because of the possibilities to integrate LED technology with other electronics-based applications such as dimmers, drivers, and Wi-Fi.
8. A year has 8,760 hours, compared to the approximately 50,000 hour life time of an LED.
9. Before becoming a black apron Coffee Master, a partner (Starbucks employee) will have gone through many hours of training (seminars, classroom sessions), tests, and demonstrations of one's coffee-related capabilities (Michelli, 2007).
10. See also Nonaka and Takeuchi (1995), who argue that the hard-to-copy and inimitable nature of tacit knowledge ("We know more than we can tell" said Polanyi, 1966) is a building block for sustainable competitive advantage.

Literature

Michelli, J.A. (2007). *The Starbucks Experience: Five Principles for Turning the Ordinary into Extraordinary*. New York: McGraw-Hill.

Nonaka, I. and H. Takeuchi (1995). *The Knowledge Creating Company: How Japanese Companies Create the Dynamics of Innovation*. New York: Oxford University Press.

Polanyi, M. (1966). *The Tacit Dimension*. New York: Doubleday.

Van Hooydonk, S. (2012). *Lighting University Performance Support Eindhoven*. Internal company document.

11

CORPORATE UNIVERSITY DEFINITIONS, LITERATURE, AND LESSONS LEARNED

> Our progress as an organization can be no
> swifter than our progress in learning.[1]

Discussion of corporate university cases, strategies, and models in this book has served the aim of coming to grips with the evolving corporate university concept, and what has been missing so far is a corporate university definition. This chapter starts with an exploration of corporate university definitions, followed by the formulation of a working definition to promote further development of the concept. Moreover, the boundaries of the corporate university concept will be explored and redefined on the basis of specific examples which show how organizational learning serves strategy at firms like IKEA, FrieslandCampina, and Ducati.

Next, a literature review helps to find out how the corporate university concept has evolved internationally over the past 15 years or so, paying particular attention to the connection between strategy and organizational learning. Strikingly, this topic has been largely neglected in the recent literature, while it receives prominent attention in contemporary corporate university reality.

The cases in this book examine the corporate universities of Mars, Deloitte, Shell, Canon, ING Bank, and Philips Lighting to learn more about how these companies build, maintain, and run them. The School, College, and Academy framework (described in Chapter 3) will be employed to analyze and discuss the strategies that these corporate universities follow. From the case analyses, it will also be possible to derive the issues of strategy specificity, corporate university mission statements, and performance measurement. These issues are likely to be relevant for leaders who want to rethink how to enhance the role of their own corporate universities as impactful drivers of performance through organizational learning.

Corporate university definitions and concepts

Through the past 15 years, practitioners and scholars have formulated a variety of definitions in attempts to grasp the concept of corporate university, and naturally, they reflect the early stage of development of this concept and its multidisciplinary nature. Table 11.1 contains a set of definitions most commonly found in the literature. All of them revolve around learning in organizations, but that is where the commonality ends.

Some of the definitions in Table 11.1 refer to general strategy (Jeanne Meister, Kevin Wheeler, and Mark Allen). Most of them describe a corporate university as an organizational entity, except for the one by Meister. John Walton narrows corporate universities down to forms of formal learning in organizations, though this may be too narrow, as informal learning has received increased attention in more recent years. Karen Gould stresses that a corporate university is an entity outside academia – probably due to the confusion that use of the term "university" in combination with "corporate" has evoked, particularly outside the USA.[2] Exemplary for past efforts to arrive at a corporate university definition is the resolution by Christopher Prince and Graham Beaver (2001) to use the term corporate university "as a convenient label or language construct" as a starting point to further explore the phenomenon.

A widely accepted and clear-cut corporate university definition does not exist. The body of knowledge about corporate universities is fragmented in nature and above all, it is still in the making. The creation of a working definition would seem

TABLE 11.1 Corporate university definitions

Definition	Source
"**The strategic umbrella** for developing and educating employees, customers, and suppliers in order to meet an organization's business strategies."	J.C. Meister (1998)
"**A function or department** that is strategically oriented toward integrating the development of people as individuals with their performance as teams and ultimately as an entire organization: by linking with suppliers, by conducting wide-ranging research, by facilitating the delivery of content, and by leading the effort to build a superior leadership team."	K. Wheeler (1998)
"**An overarching designation** for formal learning and knowledge creation activities and processes in an organization."	J. Walton (1999)
"**An educational entity that is a strategic tool** designed to assist its parent organization in achieving its mission by conducting activities that cultivate individual and organizational learning, knowledge, and wisdom."	M. Allen (2002)
"**An educational entity existing outside academia**; a companion to the concept of life-long learning, the corporate university enables businesses, both for-profit and not-for-profit, to maintain and expand the expertise of their workforces and, as a result, to secure their positions in the marketplace."	K.E. Gould (2005)

Source: Center for Strategy & Leadership research[3]

useful, however, to provide a common point of reference for future development of the concept. Drawing from the lessons learned in this book and the literature that has been available on corporate universities so far, a working definition is proposed as follows:

A corporate university is a unit, approach, or concept that supports strategy renewal, implementation, and/or optimization through organizational learning.

For the definition to be effective it is important to be clear about what is meant by "strategy" and "organizational learning," as these concepts are neither self-explanatory nor much agreed upon. In the framework of that working definition:

The word "strategy" represents *a course of action for achieving sustainable competitive advantage within the confines of an organization's purpose.*[4]

Non-commercial organizations such as NGOs, ministries, municipalities, and pressure groups tend to replace the concept of "competitive advantage" with "(optimal) societal impact or relevance."

For organizations to align with their environments, they must have the capability to learn, which is defined more precisely here:

Organizational learning is *the development of insights, knowledge, and associations between past actions, the effectiveness of those actions, and future actions that will impact the long-term survival of an organization.*[5]

Organizational learning is not seen here as the mere sum of each member's learning. Members of the organization may come and go, but meanings, memories, worldviews, capabilities, and ideologies persist at the organizational level, based on associations, cognitive systems, and memories that are shared by members of the organization (Hedberg, 1981).

The working definition deliberately leaves open if a corporate university is an organizational unit, a key component of corporate strategy (but not a unit), or a philosophy that determines how an organization differs from the competition and thrives. The way IKEA, FrieslandCampina, and Ducati connect organizational learning with strategy provides useful examples, each representing one of those three categories.

The corporate university as an organizational unit

IKEA has a corporate university in the form of an organizational unit which plays a central role in supporting strategy optimization through organizational learning. IKEA is a Swedish retailer of affordable home furnishings, and the company employed over 120,000 people worldwide in 2011, serving over 522 million customers in more than 300 stores in 41 countries.[6] More in particular, the corporate university is part of the international expansion strategy of the firm, with an average of 15 store openings per year.

"The College in the IKEA Concept Center" is the official name of this corporate university. Known as "The College" by most co-workers,[7] it is located on the premises of the IKEA Concept Center, which is actually a fully-fledged store in the

Netherlands. The concept center can be seen as the product and marketing testing grounds of the firm, where the college is a vehicle for knowledge replication and transfer. IKEA grows internationally through a franchise approach, with investors paying for and utilizing the IKEA formula to build and run their own IKEA stores. As the owner of the formula, IKEA brings franchisees from the whole world to this college to learn how to set up and run an IKEA store in all its facets. Like the IKEA flat packs, much of that knowledge is codified and standardized.

The international exploitation of the IKEA retail formula through franchising lies at the heart of the growth strategy of the firm. The College in the IKEA Concept Center serves as one of the pillars of this strategy, effectively optimizing concept replication.[8] In addition, the corporate university is instrumental in disseminating the lessons learned from testing new products as well as marketing and sales approaches in the IKEA Concept Center.

The corporate university as a key component of corporate strategy

FrieslandCampina deploys the corporate university concept to understand its own business from an external stakeholder perspective, which in turn forms an essential component for the corporate social responsibility strategy of the firm.[9] FrieslandCampina, the number 2 dairy firm in the world, with annual sales amounting to more than €10 billion and employing more than 20,000 people, is a Dutch cooperative with production facilities in 28 countries and sales in more than 100 different nations.

The firm upholds long-standing traditions which are rather inward oriented and which pay great attention to the interests of the members of the cooperative (farmers who supply milk to the organization). In recent years, the cooperative has decided to develop a corporate social responsibility strategy, and the purpose of that strategy, described in the words of FrieslandCampina's Corporate Director Sustainability & Communications, Frank van Ooijen, is

> to have a license to operate in the future.

To provide meaning and relevance to the concept of corporate social responsibility, however, the firm felt it had much to learn from external stakeholders – i.e., people affected by the activities of FrieslandCampina. "What do our stakeholders think of us? What do they find important?" These questions triggered a need for answers with regard to several themes of stakeholder interest, including nutrition, health, the natural environment, culture, and entrepreneurship. To find answers, the cooperative decided to drive an outside-in approach to organizational learning. The vehicle for organizational learning has taken the shape of an Internet-based platform for stakeholder discussions and knowledge exchange without interference by the firm. Called "The Milk Story," this platform is a portal open to anyone, created and run by an external specialist organization (quite suitably called

"Het Portaal" in Dutch) that has a reputation for independence.[10] The Milk Story website has appeared to attract thousands of stakeholders (and their "likes") who use it to share their opinions, knowledge, and questions on milk-related themes. FrieslandCampina takes lessons from it and uses them as input to shape the corporate social responsibility strategy of the cooperative. The outside-in learning approach has produced unexpected, but positive side effects. Frank van Ooijen explains:

> The platform helps FrieslandCampina to understand what is going on in our society. This understanding forms the basis to be taken seriously as a discussion partner for stakeholders such as governments and opinion leaders.

"The Milk Story" has activated and engaged a community of stakeholders who use the platform as a stepping stone for their discussions on Twitter and Facebook, and as a point of departure for contests, co-creation sessions, and other stakeholder events. This approach does not carry the name "corporate university" and is not an organizational unit. Notwithstanding this, it builds almost entirely on informal learning, user-generated content, knowledge exchange and creation, and a deliberate activation of a mutual learning community. In short, the approach boils down to outside-in organizational learning in a distinctive way, and it drives strategy renewal at FrieslandCampina.

The corporate university as a philosophy

Ducati can be examined as an example of the corporate university concept applied in a philosophy that permeates the entire firm. Organizational learning determines how this firm differs from the competition, and thrives on it. Headquartered in the Italian city of Bologna, Ducati has its own museum – but it has no corporate university.

At first glance, the company seems to be a relatively small manufacturer of sporty motorcycles with a sleek design.[11] A closer look shows a firm that is active in the worldwide business of emotion and lifestyle built around the Ducati brand, which stands for the promise of exceptional performance, design, and character. The firm is a totally network-based organization: every single component of Ducati motorcycles, equipment, and fashion merchandise is manufactured and/or co-designed by partner organizations – some even by competitors.

The company earns an important part of its competitive advantage from the way it has shaped learning from and for others outside the company. By sharing and creating new knowledge with companies such as Shell (fuel technology for combustion engines), Brembo (brakes), Bridgestone (tires), and Puma (fashion and retail knowledge), Ducati manages not only to stay ahead of powerful and much larger motorcycle manufacturers such as Honda, Yamaha, and Kawasaki, but also manages to stay ahead of competitors in the lifestyle field, and quite literally on the international race tracks. The company has more than 50 partners in a wide range of industries, also including computer companies and fashion houses. As CEO Gabriele del Torchio summarizes concisely:

> We are a small company with not much more than 1,000 people on the payroll. We do not have the same budgets as the Japanese giants. That is why we need to work closely with partners in our network in order to be competitive.[12]

The inter-organizational learning approach works here, because Ducati can offer something to its cooperative partners that is unique and hard to copy. The firm provides the ultimate place for knowledge innovation in the fields of technology, marketing, and e-commerce. In essence, Ducati does not have a corporate university, but acts as if it were just that for a network of partners. Ducati Corse, the part of the company that focuses on the international racing competitions (Moto GP and Superbike World Championship), is a good example of this ideology. Based on a Harvard Business School study, Francesca Gino and Gary Pisano (2011) designated Ducati Corse as an exemplary learning organization that works according to the principle "If it ain't broke, experiment." The philosophy behind this principle is that success can offer learning experiences, just as failures do. Ducati and its partners learn continuously from each other's successes and failures – on and around the race track.

The art of inter-organizational learning at Ducati has been honed over many years. What the cooperative partners learn from their partnership with Ducati is likely to be accessible to the competition within a year. By that time, however, Ducati will already be another step ahead of them. It is safe to say that the company thrives on its capability not only to bring speed to the motorbikes it builds, but also to organizational learning.

In sum, Ducati neither has a corporate university unit, nor does it deploy the corporate university concept as a key component of a broader corporate strategy. The firm's activities in the manner of a corporate university are instrumental to knowledge creation for a network of leading companies, and that is in turn the keystone of Ducati's competitive strength.

The corporate university literature

Scholarly literature on corporate universities is still relatively scarce. Publications by practitioners are available in a larger number, but not very abundantly. The corporate university concept has a history of more than two decades, though. In particular, a clear connection between organizational learning and strategy can be traced back to the seminal work by Peter Senge, with *The Fifth Discipline* (1990) as the most commonly known publication. Learning is explicitly linked to vision, i.e., a desired long-term future, which can be seen as the cornerstone of emergent strategy, or further strategy specification.[13] This refers to the essence of strategy for companies: A quest for the achievement of sustainable competitive advantage. Moreover, Senge, inspired by Arie de Geus from Royal Dutch Shell, asserts the following:

> Only organizations that are able to learn faster than their competitors will be leading in the future.

In the 1990s, after the "learning organization" had been embraced by a broad and worldwide audience of senior managers, the road ahead seemed to have been cleared for the development of the corporate university concept. In tune, literature on corporate universities began to gain traction in the late 1990s – starting in the USA. The body of knowledge on corporate universities has been increasing since then, albeit not at a steady pace. Publications concerning corporate universities reached a high at the turn of the millennium, with books and journal articles from authors in different countries, including those of the American Jeanne Meister (1998), the Dutch Martyn Rademakers and Nicoline Huizinga (2000), the British Richard Dealtry (2001), the French Annick Renaud-Coulon (2002), and the American Mark Allen (2002). After that, publications on corporate universities seemed to ebb away, until a new peak appeared in 2005 with a special issue of the *Journal of Workplace Learning*, various handbooks and manuals of British origin by Paton et al. (2005) as well as Wheeler and Clegg (2005), and the initiation of research supported by the European Science Foundation.

A third wave of attention for the corporate university concept began near the end of the past decade, mainly from the practitioner and consultant perspectives of Allen (2007), Sham (2007), Renaud-Coulon (2008), and Qiao (2009). The resulting literature has not been particularly focused in nature, covering a plethora of learning-related topics ranging from e-learning and wisdom to creating corporate university brands. Along with those publications, the number of blogs, websites, and community forums about corporate universities has been steadily expanding. In comparison, scholarly research into corporate universities has remained scarce. This seems to be in part due to the multidisciplinary nature of the concept, which makes it difficult for an ongoing discourse to evolve in this field.[14] In the meantime, corporate universities continue to develop within and between organizations on all continents, most prominently in the USA, Western Europe, and Russia, but also in emerging economies such as China.

Publications about corporate universities have focused predominantly on learning in organizations thus far. How exactly organizational learning drives strategy remains largely unexplored or unclear. This seems to be a blind spot in the literature, though the provision of clear contributions to strategy is the lifeblood of many corporate universities today. After more than two decades, the message of Peter Senge (1990) and Arie de Geus[15] about the strategic relevance of speedy learning still holds true, and deserves more attention. The speed of learning, however, is not the only key dimension relevant to the achievement of competitive advantage and/or societal impact. As is demonstrated by the case-based chapters in this book, the direction of organizational learning is at least as important. The case descriptions call for further analysis in order to shed more light on what corporate universities can do to shape their roles as the drivers of learning organizations.

The strategic role of corporate universities

The corporate universities of Mars, Deloitte, Shell, Canon, ING Bank, and Philips Lighting that are described in this book provide clear and direct support to the strategy of their parent organizations. The School–College–Academy (SCA) framework presented in Chapter 3 will be used below as an instrument to analyze, interpret, and characterize the strategic positions taken by the corporate universities in their parent organizations. The strategic positions are dynamic in nature, and the cases of Mars, Shell, and ING show in particular that corporate university strategies shift between the School, College, and Academy types over time – along with the needs of their parent organizations.

Mars University

Mars University passed through several stages of development before arriving at its present form. Figure 11.1 provides an overview of this process in terms of the SCA framework.

The corporate university activities and priorities described in the case seem to resemble an inclination to the School strategy. For instance, in tune with a School strategy, the *Mars Academy in China* provides the company with a competitive edge through a formal education program that ensures higher skill levels at Mars, and also loyalty, in comparison to the competition.

One could argue that Mars University became engaged in a College strategy as of 2004, when corporate learning was adopted by senior management as an

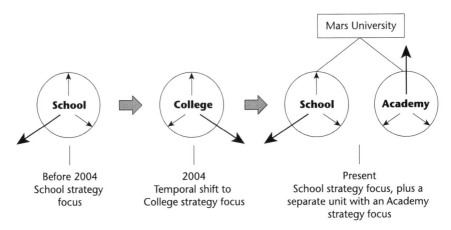

FIGURE 11.1 Shifting corporate university strategies at Mars University

Source: Analysis by the author

instrument for corporate restructuring and organizational development was considered key to realigning Mars business activities with the environment. The new, profit center based corporate structure at Mars demanded new management and leadership capabilities from the people who had to make the new strategy work, including the realization of cross-unit synergies.

Given the temporal nature of the Mars transformation, the center of gravity of Mars University soon shifted to a School strategy again. With an emphasis on consolidation, uniformity, and cost reduction of educational programs, also focusing on operational performance and capability development, the School strategy has remained dominant at the large, multi-unit, and global organization that Mars University has grown into. The development in this direction can be seen in the light of Mars as a company that competes on the basis of relatively stable business systems for value creation in the worldwide confectionery, food, and pet food markets.

Notwithstanding this, a new unit was established recently, which is called the "Customized Learning Group", and resembles the Academy-type strategy ambitions. It has been designated to help the company address and solve business challenges through organizational learning. Moreover, a program called "Leading in Unprecedented Times" focuses on the key debates, tensions, and strategic choices that face Mars in the future. Though these activities are all relatively minor in comparison with the vast range of School-type programs offered by Mars University, any business will need to strike a balance between exploitation and exploration. Mars also needs exceptional learning, and the Customized Learning Group as well as the Mars University leadership program seem to cater to this need.

ING Business School – ING Bank Academy

Like Mars University, ING Business School (IBS) has passed through different generic strategies. Starting as a School-type corporate university in 1998 when they taught banking skills and insurance related topics, IBS shifted towards a College strategy in 2003. A new corporate strategy aimed at international expansion required a transformation of the company, covering not only structures, systems, and culture, but also, and perhaps even particularly, leadership capabilities. IBS was placed in a position to help disseminate the new strategy and enable ING Group managers and functional specialists to actually implement it. As time progressed, the nature of the corporate university strategy at IBS gradually shifted back to a curriculum-based School approach based on "pull" (i.e., direct demand) from the business units. This was in alignment with a corporate strategy that shifted from transformation towards an exploitation strategy again. Because there was also a need for exceptional learning to drive strategy exploration for the ING Group, an Academy-type activity in the form of quarterly dialogue series between managers from the divisions and executive board members became part of the IBS repertoire of services.

What is more interesting is the rapid shift back to a College strategy when the ING Group was severely hurt by the global financial crisis. The need for curriculum-based programs virtually vanished, while the need for tailored interventions in the

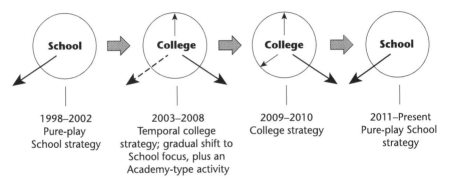

FIGURE 11.2 Generic strategies of ING Business School and ING Bank Academy

Source: Analysis by the author

field of leadership came in demand. Transformation was back on top of the management agenda as the ING Group engaged in a deep, broad, and fast restructuring program that, among other things, resulted in a split of the company into separate bank and insurance companies. The shift towards a College strategy by IBS materialized through the concept of mass customization: elements from the IBS curriculum were used as building blocks for (mass-)customized transformational leadership programs on demand.

While the existence of IBS came to an end, being decimated to save costs, the corporate university emerged again in another form, as the ING Bank Academy. Much of the time, ING Bank Academy resembles the IBS that was established as a "School" in 1998, though much smaller now and certainly without a chateau as the backdrop. One could argue that, seen from a generic strategy perspective depicted in Figure 11.2, the corporate university has come full circle.

Shell Project Academy

Royal Dutch Shell established the Shell Project Academy (SPA) in 2005 as part of a series of measures that were undertaken to revitalize the corporate strategy. The aim of the company was to re-establish a sustainable competitive position in the development of hydrocarbon reserves for business partners in the international oil and gas industry. The role of SPA was to build and sustain a large corps of managers with excellent project management capabilities. Building this corps was one of the keys needed for the strategy revitalization to succeed, which must be seen in the light of the importance and complexity of project management in the oil and gas industry. Projects aimed to find and bring new hydrocarbon reserves into production take investments ranging from US$ 50 million to US$ 20 billion, with lead times of five to ten years.

The establishment of SPA has been effected in tune with the College strategy – project-based, and driving transformation. The project of building SPA was realized in a way that – quite appropriately – resembles project management excellence.

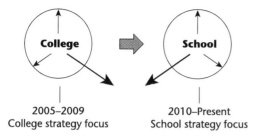

FIGURE 11.3 Shell Project Academy generic strategies over time
Source: Analysis by the author

One could argue that in this US$ 40 million investment project little has been left to the element of surprise. Thoughtfully, however, also ambiguity was built into the system in the form of an SPA governance structure that requires constructive leadership to function well, rather than an operational management attitude.

SPA has grown into a corporate university that helps to build and develop the competences of an entire (project) community in support of company objectives. The community, in turn, is part of an integrated system for organizational learning. The system, known as the SPA Pentagon, connects community building with competence and career development, mentoring and coaching, assessment and accreditation, and a course portfolio.

Projects are supposed to have a clear beginning and end. The project of establishing SPA, which led to organizational development in support of strategy revitalization at Royal Dutch Shell, took about four years. The corporate strategy revitalization process at Royal Dutch Shell was successful, and the company embarked on new strategic initiatives led by a new CEO. SPA can be seen to have shifted towards the generic School-type strategy, as building and developing the corps of project management has become "learning as usual" in support of the strategy to stay abreast of the competition in the quest for access to new oil and gas reserves. Figure 11.3 provides an image of the SPA generic corporate university strategies over time.

SPA, together with other organizational learning activities at Royal Dutch Shell, form the equivalent of an *avant garde* corporate university in the oil and gas industry. It is telling that large international and state-owned companies like, for instance, Kuwait Petroleum, Pertamina (Indonesia), Petronas (Malaysia), and Gazprom (Russia) have followed suit and invested substantially in building their own corporate universities.[16]

Canon Academy

The Canon Academy of Canon Europe, based in London, can be taken as a specific example of a pure-play College-strategy corporate university. Senior management deploys Canon Academy to keep the company up to speed through fast and comprehensive strategy implementation in a rapidly changing business environment. Accordingly, learning-driven change and development are the common thread in all projects of this corporate university.

Canon competes in the international imaging industry, which is characterized by extremely high-pace technological developments and very short time-to-market cycles. Product life cycles (i.e., a product being replaced by a newer and better one) as short as two months are no exception. This explains why the pace of learning at Canon must be high, too. It is in this organizational context that Canon Academy emerged as a driver of transformational learning. The "high-speed" learning capabilities initially developed by Canon Academy to support the company by keeping knowledge and competences up to date – which can be typified as a School strategy – are likely to have paved the way towards developing and honing the contemporary transformational learning services.

The Canon global strategy can be described as moving away from an imaging hardware company towards an integrated imaging hardware, software, and service organization. Through the Canon Academy, the European division of Canon is capable of cascading this global strategy into strategies that are further specified and implemented in regional and local markets. It is the role of the corporate university to support managers and employees in finding out how to implement strategy in the context of market demands, moves of competitors, and the organizational reality at Canon. Canon Academy provides the necessary contacts, experts, platforms, methods, tools, and techniques to empower them to do this via the path of organizational learning. More in particular, implementation teams are configured with the help of the corporate university, and team processes are facilitated by organizational learning experts from Canon Academy. They support the people involved in specifying and developing the roles, responsibilities, organizational structures and processes, and the competencies that are needed to make the strategy work.

An important asset Canon Academy has developed to fulfill its strategic role is a network of daily contacts across the entire organization. In this sense, one could picture the corporate university as an antenna for management and leadership issues in the organization. Another asset is the regular and direct contact with senior management, which is rooted in the organizational structure of the company. All management teams include a member who represents the Canon Academy – a total of 12 senior managers. Speaking in terms of assets – or better said, no assets – the corporate university does not "own" any curricula, programs, content, or implementation processes that it helps to build. The ownership resides with top management.

The Canon Academy has a clear image of its strategic focus: the corporate university team members limit themselves to providing support and advice on the crossroads of strategy implementation and organizational learning. In short, as depicted in Figure 11.4, Canon Academy pursues a predominant College strategy to fulfill the task of enabling people in the organization to learn what they need in order to continuously specify and implement new strategy.

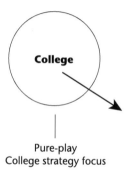

FIGURE 11.4   Generic strategy of Canon Academy
Source: Analysis by the author

Deloitte University

The relatively young Deloitte University (DU) was built 2011 near Dallas, Texas in the USA as a School-type corporate university. At DU a broad range of state-of-the-art approaches and innovative technologies in the field of individual and organizational learning are deployed to support the Deloitte "As One" strategy.

The strategic role and impact of Deloitte University can be understood best if placed against the backdrop of its parent organization Deloitte, which is one of the largest professional services firms in the world. The firm can be considered to be both a single entity and fragmented at the same time. Under the Deloitte banner, more than 193,000 professionals in 48 independent member firms in 153 countries and regions collaborate to provide audit, consulting, financial advisory, risk management, and tax services. Needless to say, professional development is of great importance to a firm like Deloitte. Accordingly, reaping and leveraging the benefits of clout and economies of scale and scope with regard to organizational learning are competitive imperatives for the firm.

The "As One" strategy of Deloitte is a broadly defined growth strategy providing guidance to the member firms. DU has set out to develop a global curriculum that is instrumental to ensuring that sufficient numbers of employees acquire the technical, industry, professional, and leadership skills and knowledge required for the growth strategy to succeed.

In tune with the principles of a School strategy (depicted in Figure 11.5), DU makes relevant knowledge available to a geographically and professionally widely dispersed organization. Keywords from the case description which pinpoint the nature of the corporate university activities are *consistency, unity, standards, principles, global,* and *one*. All of these keywords have a connotation of standardizing organizational learning – as far as possible and desirable, and through the collaboration of a great number of stakeholders in the large and international firm that Deloitte is. Clearly, balancing between global standardization and local adaptation of organizational learning is an art mastered at Deloitte University.

FIGURE 11.5 Generic strategy of Deloitte University

Source: Analysis by the author

Philips Lighting University

At first glance, Philips Lighting University seems to follow a School-type strategy with many innovative twists. Closer scrutiny reveals a College strategy, flirting with activities that resemble an Academy approach. Philips Lighting is a leading firm in the market for light technology, employing approximately 54,000 people worldwide.

Philips Lighting University offers a series of courses revolving around LED technology. One of the twists is that employees can earn certificates that enhance their status in the organization. This has resulted in unprecedented global demand for the courses throughout the firm, with more than 10,000 certificates granted in the year that the program was launched. The knowledge and information relevant to the courses is attractive and easily accessible through online (and mobile) learning offers featuring videos, games, webinars, e-books, self-study e-learning packages, and product wikis. It is up to the people taking the courses to choose which sources to use before taking a test for certification.

Although the corporate university curriculum seems to reflect a School-type strategy, it is focused on transformational learning that affects the entire firm and many of its business partners. Philips Lighting University originates from the top management vision that organizational learning is a key competitive component in times of industry-level system change. The firm faces changing rules of the game in this industry, a development that is driven by the rise of LED technology.[17]

Philips Lighting is taking advantage of rapid organizational learning to help make sense of the revolutionary changes confronting the firm, distributors, installation companies, and also industrial users and consumers. The College strategy of Philips Lighting University can be summarized as realigning both knowledge and learning capabilities of the firm and its partners with the new industrial reality of Philips Lighting – on a global scale. According to Stefaan van Hooydonk, dean of the corporate university, a prerequisite for success is to move away from

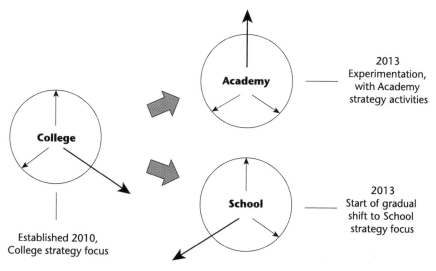

FIGURE 11.6 SCA strategies of Philips Lighting University
Source: Analysis by the author

traditional thinking in terms of curricula, courses, and classrooms within the borders of an organization. To make transformational learning work, thinking should be in terms of bringing speed to knowledge across the entire industry ecosystem. This is precisely what Philips Lighting University is doing. Around the world, tens of thousands of people within and around the organization are being enabled to learn in the way they prefer most, with access to a broad range of Internet-based self-study propositions.

It is only a question of time before the new industrial rules of the game that Philips Lighting is becoming aligned with will turn into accepted industrial wisdom. Likewise, the transformational nature of organizational learning driven by Philips Lighting University will gradually become learning as usual. Philips Lighting University is not likely to sit still in the meantime. Academy strategy ambitions are reflected in explorations, since 2013, by the corporate university into the uncharted waters of informal learning supported, for example, by digital technology. The efforts of Philips Lighting University to break down barriers and allow informal knowledge to flow through the firm may prove helpful for Philips Lighting to out-innovate the competition. Figure 11.6 provides an overview of the generic strategies seen at Philips Lighting since 2010.

Comparing and contrasting corporate universities

A process of comparing and contrasting Mars University, Deloitte University, Shell Project Academy, Canon Academy, ING Bank Academy, and Philips Lighting University reveals three strategic issues for corporate university strategy that go beyond their generic strategies. Commonalities and differences that catch the eye are the degrees in which their strategies have been specified, the degrees to which their missions are clear, and how they keep track of performance.[18] These three issues reflect the leadership challenge of actually moving the organization (in this case the corporate university) in the desired strategic direction (Cyert, 1990; Stacey, 1993; Meyer, 2007 and 2013).

Strategy specification: Vision or Blueprint?

The strategies of the six corporate universities described vary greatly with regard to the amount of detail they provide. Some are very broad, others quite specific. Figure 2.5 (in Chapter 2) depicts five different levels of strategy specificity, ranging from a vision (a broad picture of a desired long-term future) to a strategic blueprint (a very specific plan). The underlying idea is that less detailed strategies offer more leeway to cope with situations characterized by unpredictability and complexity. Providing less detail, however, also comes with the need to empower people to explore and find out by themselves what to do along the way. Conversely, highly specified strategies can provide much clarity about the direction to take, including actions to take, roles to fulfill and commitments to keep. Detailed plans, however, may suffer from the pitfalls of inflexibility and wrong assumptions about future developments, and they may hamper initiative.

From the six cases, Shell Project Academy and Mars University can be seen as corporate universities with detailed strategies. The Shell Project Academy strategy is, by far, the most detailed one in comparison to the other five corporate universities. The SPA strategy specifies among others the five corporate university activities (summarized in a Pentagon figure), the target groups, curricula, the number of seats in the programs per year, and budgets involved.[19] The dominant strategy perspective at Shell Project Academy is clear: first think and design, then implement and, if needed, make adjustments. Mars University follows a similar approach to strategy specification, with attention for details of the curricula content, governance structures, administration and reporting systems, and budgets among other items. The strategy of Deloitte University seems less specified in comparison with Mars University and the Shell Project Academy. The DU strategy is likely to be less detailed in order to provide the leeway required to constantly align with the needs of a fluid and diverse organizational environment.

By contrast, Canon Academy yields the picture of guidance by a robust strategy that, perhaps counter-intuitively, has not been specified in great detail. What is clear, however, is that the learning specialists of Canon Academy are empowered to contribute to strategy implementation in a volatile Canon organization. In a similar vein, Philips Lighting University is vision-led (bringing speed to knowledge, in all possible ways), and definitely not blueprinted. This corporate university strategy is explorative in nature, to spur innovative forms of organizational learning.

ING Bank Academy is engaged in a strategic re-orientation process and confronted with many uncertainties, which leaves little room for high levels of

FIGURE 11.7 Comparing and contrasting strategy specificity
Source: Analysis by the author

strategy specification. Its predecessor, ING Business School, always leaned toward an emergent strategy following a step by step approach to shape and renew its business system within the boundaries of its mandate, yet allowing for experimentation and exploration for more than a decade. A summary of the outcomes of comparing and contrasting the six cases in this book with regard to strategy specificity is depicted in Figure 11.7.

How to achieve a clear strategic profile?

Many corporate universities suffer from the lack of a clear strategic profile in the organization. As described in the Mars University case, for example, a review in 2010 revealed that members of the parent organization were uncertain as to who (and what) Mars University was for. At present, Mars University, but also Deloitte University, Shell Project Academy, Canon Academy, and Philips Lighting University benefit from a clear profile in their parent organizations. As depicted in Figure 11.8, a persuasive mission statement is helpful to achieve that profile, but regular and direct links with top management and strong brand images appear to be important factors, too.

The profiles of Deloitte University, Philips Lighting University, and Shell Project Academy are supported by corporate university mission statements.[20] Deloitte University operates under the banner "To grow the world's best leaders." Philips Lighting University is widely known in the organization – and beyond – as an "Accelerator Bringing Speed to Knowledge." Shell Project Academy maintains the credo "We can no longer afford to learn solely from our own mistakes." It also has a strong logo (the SPA Pentagon) and invests substantial efforts in communication through roadshow presentations, posters, newsletters, and its website.

To the organizational members of Canon Europe – and more in particular top management – it is clear that Canon Academy drives organizational change through learning, and helps to keep knowledge and competences up to date. The direct contact with top management on a regular basis seems to play an important role in maintaining this profile. The same can be said of ING Business School up to the time when radical changes hit the parent organization. Mars University seems to benefit from its efforts to build a strong brand name in the organization, putting all

FIGURE 11.8 Shaping factors for a strategic corporate university profile

Source: Analysis by the author

learning and development within Mars under a single banner.[21] Likewise, Shell Project Academy benefits from its SPA Pentagon brand image, and Philips Lighting University has become a household name as a result of deliberate marketing efforts and, of course, living up to the promise of the brand.

Tracking performance: Indicative or comprehensive measurement?

There is great variation in the way the here described corporate universities keep track of performance. Figure 11.9 shows their relative positions on a continuum from indicative to comprehensive performance measurement.

Compared to the other corporate universities, Shell Project Academy is strikingly comprehensive where it comes to performance measurement. They track eight "main leading cost indicators" and two "contributing performance indicators,"[22]

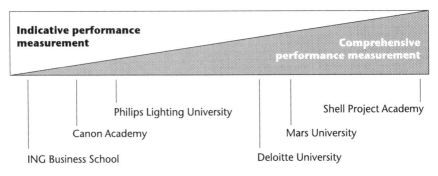

FIGURE 11.9 Variation in performance tracking styles of the corporate universities

Source: Analysis by the author

and after careful consideration, they have rejected Return on Investment as a measurement parameter. The Mars University case shows that they use performance and output metrics as part of the management system. Deloitte University keeps track of metrics such as the number of participants in its programs, learning hours spent, industry sectors represented, and the percentage of courses delivered by Deloitte people.

Philips Lighting University works with a small selection of telling performance indicators, including the number of visits to the corporate university website, the average time spent by visitors at the website, and the number of certificates earned. All indicators are attuned to the "pull" philosophy of this corporate university, and they boil down to output control. The Canon Academy case does not reveal much about performance measurement, but it is clear that the corporate university makes sure that its activities are well aligned with the performance management system of the company, which is managed by objectives.

ING Business School has always been eager to measure the effects of its programs on the business. An important indicator has become known as Return on Engagement, which revolves around the degree to which employees feel involved with the company.[23] Employee engagement builds on organizational learning for the knowledge, skills, motivation, experience, rewards, and passion which ensure that people in the company "can do, want to do, and are inspired." A generally accepted idea is that employee engagement promotes productivity and quality, which in turn furthers Return on Investment. The engagement effects of the ING Business School programs have been derived from a broad, annual, and company-wide survey covering a range of measures related to organizational culture and performance.

The corporate universities described here have in common that important elements of their performance measures are based on output control. Measures for throughput control are likely to be integrated in the learning management systems (LMS) used by some, while input measures seem to be virtually absent. It is relevant to point out here that Philips Lighting University has done away with its LMS, while other corporate universities have just begun to embrace such automated learning systems. Whatever performance measures are used, they always need to support corporate university leaders in striking a balance between control and empowerment to arrive at both effective and efficient organizational learning.

Directions for future research

In the midst of the growing relevance of corporate universities in the world, more research is needed to gain better insight in the workings of corporate universities. Case-based research and cross-national comparative research seem to be appropriate approaches to the illumination of this yet relatively new area of organizational theory and practice. The organizational systems of corporate universities and the capabilities required of those who lead them are also areas of attention.

Case-based research. Case descriptions about corporate universities have been and will remain an important source for the exploration, development, and dissemination of knowledge about the corporate university concept. Case study research is particularly well suited to understanding and building theory for complex organizational phenomena (Eisenhardt, 1989; Yin, 1994) such as corporate universities in their idiosyncratic organizational, industrial, and national context. Much can still be learned from the questions and dilemmas faced by corporate universities, as well as their innovations and practical inventions.

Cross-national comparative research. Little cross-national comparative research has been undertaken with corporate universities as yet. The relevance of this type of research is evident, regarding the fact that traditions, systems, and solutions for organizational learning vary greatly from country to country. Moreover, the national context of an organization influences the way in which companies develop and organize their competitive skills (Whitley, 2007), including organizational learning. For corporate universities it means that approaches to corporate learning which prove to work well in the home market may not be very effective abroad – and vice versa. Hence, a set of questions worth exploration by internationally operating corporate universities can be formulated as follows: How can advantage be gained from balancing between global-for-global, global-for-local, local-for-local, and local-for-global corporate university approaches?

Corporate university organizational systems. The cases and concepts in this book have paid some, but yet little attention to the organizational systems that underpin corporate university strategies. As explained in Chapter 2, organizational systems cover elements such as formal and informal structures, processes, culture, and leadership. It is likely that School, College, and Academy strategies (explained in Chapter 3) make specific demands on the configuration of organizational systems. In addition, large companies of the caliber of Mars, Philips, and Shell, but also large and small (semi-)governmental organizations have been known to face the challenge of creating synergies between their different corporate university units through integration (Rademakers, 2012). Desired benefits are higher efficiency (by eliminating duplication), economies of scale, and greater impact (through the achievement of critical mass). The challenge is to align and sometimes to merge corporate universities that often differ in nature, and to achieve this without hampering their (local) responsiveness. Research is needed to learn what fruitful routes of integration exist, which instruments are relevant, and what challenges can be anticipated.

Conclusions

Every day, across the world, thousands of organizations develop and utilize their corporate universities. In the midst of the dynamics of social and demographic shifts, technological developments, emerging economies, but also stagnation, there are more reasons than ever for firms, institutions, and governments to take advantage of corporate universities. Seen in this light, it is also an encouraging thought that few areas of organizational theory and practice are as highly receptive to discovery and knowledge sharing across organizational and national borders as the field of corporate universities is. The way this book has been realized can be seen as the ultimate proof.

What are corporate universities? How do they fulfill their strategic role? Which strategic issues and leadership questions do corporate universities need to address in order to enhance their impact on organizations they serve? These questions have been explored and discussed in this chapter, with an eye toward corporate university impact and needs for future research.

Over the past 15 years, corporate universities have taken the shape of units run like a business, but they have also emerged as approaches and philosophies that further the competitive strength of organizations through learning. Moreover, strategies followed by corporate universities differ, and over time they tend to shift towards learning as usual, transformational learning or exceptional learning, or the other way around. Clearly, there is no single best way to build, develop, and run corporate universities. The issues faced by corporate university leaders when connecting strategy and organizational learning have much in common, though.

Modern corporate universities support firms and institutions in renewing, implementing, and optimizing their strategies through rapid organizational learning in the desired direction. A new generation of senior managers has experienced the impact of corporate university programs from the start of their careers. They are likely to be the new corporate university advocates, as no one needs to explain to them the strategic relevance of organizational learning.

Notes

1. Variation by the author of a quote from John F. Kennedy (1917–63), former president of the USA. The original quote is: "Our progress as a nation can be no swifter than our progress in education."
2. Many corporate universities in continental Europe, for instance, are known as "corporate academies." Reason is that the word "university" has a strong connotation with (often tax money funded) institutions which exist to pursue fundamental research for the common good, and which provide academic (theory-based) education. Although the term corporate university has become widely accepted, to many the combination of "corporate" and "university" still sounds like a contradiction.
3. The research included an extensive exploration of university library databases and Internet sources by Giancarlo Stanco and Lotte Humme (Center for Strategy & Leadership).
4. This definition builds on the works of Porter (1980; 1996) and Meyer (2007). The concept of purpose used here is about the question why the organization exists, which is also referred to as (a component of) the mission of an organization (Meyer, 2007).
5. This definition builds on the works of Hedberg (1981), and Fiol and Lyles (1985).
6. Source: http://www.statisticbrain.com/ikea-statistics (accessed in July 2013).
7. At IKEA, the term "co-worker" refers to all people on the payroll.
8. "The College" at IKEA fits most closely to the school-type corporate university strategy (see Chapter 3 for a discussion of generic corporate university strategies).
9. FrieslandCampina also operates a corporate university called FrieslandCampina Academy, which is an organizational unit that provides a curriculum of courses to the employees of the cooperative.

10 The Dutch-language platform can be accessed and explored at www.milkstory.nl.
11 In the past decades, Ducati has been owned by Italian families (e.g., the Castiglioni family) and investment companies (e.g., Texas Pacific Group). In 2012 the German car manufacturer Audi acquired Ducati for approximately US$1.1 billion.
12 Source: case study "Ducati: Riding with the Pack" by M. Rademakers and R. Meyer in the book *Strategy Synthesis* (2010).
13 See also the explanation of Figure 2.5 in Chapter 2 of this book.
14 Scholarly research is subject to institutional arrangements governing the allocation of resources and rewards, and to connections with non-scientific audiences (Whitley, 2000). The nature of these arrangements seems to hinder the adoption of the corporate university concept in the social system of academic knowledge production.
15 In Peter Senge's book *The Fifth Discipline*, reference is made to a quote from Arie de Geus (former head of planning for Royal Dutch Shell): "The ability to learn faster than your competitors may be the only sustainable competitive advantage" (Senge, 1990: 4).
16 Kuwait Petroleum Corporation has set up and runs a corporate university (Q8 Academy) that is located in Western Europe. The mission statement of the company points out that the company "wishes to grow into a learning organization." The corporate university – following a School strategy – started to develop in 2009 and won an award in 2012.
17 LED technology is replacing light bulbs and fluorescent light sources. As LEDs are electronic components emitting light, rather than lamps, the rules of the game in the lighting industry are shifting towards those of the electronics industry with, among other effects, short product life cycles.
18 For practical reasons, corporate universities are seen here as organizational units, which is in line with the nature of the corporate universities described in the six presented cases.
19 It must be noted here that the case in this book does not cover all details of the strategy.
20 A mission statement should not be confused with the mission of an organization. Mission statements are generally meant to communicate to the outside world, in a concise manner, why an organization exists. An organizational mission is much more detailed, covering for example norms, values, and beliefs, and it can be informal in nature.
21 Source: http://www.corpu.com/research/mars-inc-case-study-business-outcomes-impacted-new-university-brand/ (posted April 2013, accessed July 2013).
22 See Figure 3.3 in Chapter 3 for details.
23 This measure is not described in the ING Business School/ING Bank Academy case here. A description of the measure can be found in the case "Evolutie van een Corporate University," Rademakers, 2012.

Literature

Allen, M. (ed.) (2007). *The Next Generation of Corporate Universities*. San Francisco: Pfeiffer.
— (2002). *The Corporate University Handbook*. Amacom Press.
Charan, R., S. Drotter, and J. Noel (2001). *The Leadership Pipeline: How to Build the Leadership Powered Company*. San Francisco: Jossey-Bass.
Cross, J. (2007). *Informal Learning: Rediscovering the Natural Pathways that Inspire Innovation and Performance*. San Francisco: Pfeiffer.
Cyert, R.M. (1990). *Defining Leadership and Explicating the Process*. San Francisco: Jossey-Bass.
Dealtry, R. (2001). *The Corporate University Blueprint: Managing Corporate Learning*. Birmingham: Dynamic SWOT Associates.
Eisenhardt, K.M. (1989). Building Theories from Case Study Research. *Academy of Management Review*. Vol. 14, No. 4, pp. 532–50.
Fiol and Lyles (1985), Organizational Learning. *Academy of Management Review*, Vol. 10, No. 4, pp. 803–13.

Gino, F. and G.P. Pisano (2011). Why Leaders Don't Learn from Success. *Harvard Business Review*, Vol. 89, No. 4, pp. 68–74.

Gould, K.E. (2005). The Corporate University: A Model for Sustaining an Expert Workforce in the Human Services. *Behaviour Modification*, Vol. 29, No. 3, pp. 508–20.

Hedberg, B. (1981). How Organizations Learn and Unlearn? In P.C. Nystrom and W.H. Starbuck (eds.). *Handbook of Organizational Design*. London: Oxford University Press.

Martin, R. (2007). *The Opposable Mind: How Successful Leaders Win through Integrative Thinking*. Cambridge, MA: Harvard Business School Publishing.

Meister, J.C. (1998). *Corporate Universities: Lessons in Building a World-Class Workforce*. New York: McGraw-Hill.

Meyer, R. (2007). *Mapping the Mind of the Strategist: A Quantitative Methodology for Measuring the Strategic Beliefs of Executives*. Rotterdam: ERIM Ph.D. Series Research in Management 106.

— (2013). *The Paradox of Control and Empowerment*. Discussion document. Rotterdam: Center for Strategy & Leadership.

Paton, R., S. Taylor, J. Storey and G. Peters (eds.) (2005). *Handbook of Corporate University Development: Managing Strategic Learning Initiatives in Public and Private Domains*. Aldershot: Gower.

Porter, M.E. (1980). *Competitive Strategy: Techniques for Analyzing Competitors and Industries*. New York: The Free Press.

— (1996). What is Strategy? *Harvard Business Review*, Vol. 74, No. 6. pp. 1–19.

Prince, C. and G. Beaver (2001). The Rise and Rise of the Corporate University: The Emerging Corporate Learning Agenda. *International Journal of Management Education*, Vol. 1, No. 2, pp. 7–26.

Qiao, J. X. (2009). Corporate Universities in China: Processes, Issues and Challenges. *Journal of Workplace Learning*, Vol. 21, No. 2, pp. 166–74.

Rademakers, M. and N. Huizinga (2000). How Strategic is Your Corporate University? *New Corporate University Review*, Vol. 6, No. 6, pp. 18–23.

Rademakers, M. (2005). Corporate Universities: Driving Force of Knowledge Innovation. *Journal of Workplace Learning*, Vol. 17, No. 1, pp. 130–36.

— (2012). *Corporate Universities: Aanjagers van de Lerende Organisatie*. Deventer: Kluwer.

Rademakers, M. and R. Meyer. (2010). Ducati: Riding with the Pack. In De Wit, B. and R.J.H. Meyer (eds.). *Strategy Synthesis: Resolving Strategy Paradoxes to Create Competitive Advantage*, 3rd edition. London: Cengage.

Renaud-Coulon, A. (2008). *Corporate Universities: A Lever of Corporate Responsibility*. Paris: Global CCU Publisher.

— (2002). *Universités d'entreprise, vers une Mondialisation de L'intelligence*. Paris: Village Mondial-Pearson Education.

Senge, P. (1990). *The Fifth Discipline: The Art & Practice of the Learning Organization*. New York: Doubleday.

Seufert, S. and I. Diesner (2010). *Trendstudy 2010: Mapping Future Trends for Corporate Learning and Development*. Swiss Centre for Innovations in Learning, University of St. Gallen.

Sham, C. (2007). An Exploratory Study of Corporate Universities in China. *Journal of Workplace Learning*, Vol. 19, No. 4, pp. 257–64.

Stacey, R. (1993). Strategy as Order Emerging from Chaos. *Long Range Planning*, Vol. 26, No. 1, pp. 23–29.

Tappscot, D. and A.D. Williams (2006). *Wikinomics: How Mass Collaboration Changes Everything*. New York: Penguin.

Walton, J. (1999). Human Resource Development and the Corporate University. In J. Walton, (ed.), *Strategic Human Resource Development*, pp. 412–37. London: Pearson Education.

Wheeler, K. (1998). *The Uses and Misuses of the Term "Corporate University."* Global Learning: http://www.kwheeler.com/whatcu.htm.

Wheeler, K. and E. Clegg (2005). *The Corporate University Workbook: Launching the 21st Century Learning Organization*. San Francisco: Pfeiffer.

Whitley, R. (2000). *The Intellectual and Social Organization of the Sciences*, 2nd edition. New York: Oxford University Press.

— (2007). *Business Systems and Organizational Capabilities: The Institutional Structuring of Competitive Competences*. Oxford: Oxford University Press.

Yin, R. (1994). *Case Study Research: Design and Methods*, 2nd edition. Thousand Oaks, CA: Sage Publications.

INDEX

Academy strategy 25–6, 28–35, 134–5, 141, 146
accreditation 84, 89–90, 137
Achmea Academy 29
Agfa HealthCare 7, 114, 116–17, 124, 125, 126n5
agility 16, 64, 75–6
Ahold 4, 45, 46–7, 48
alignment: business and market 11–13, 23, 24; business and organization 13–16; ING Business School 106, 107; Mars University 61, 62; organization and individual 17, 18–19; performance management systems 101
Allen, Mark 128, 133
Alliantie Academie 29–31
Amazon 36n15
ambidexterity 26, 35n3
analytics 73
APM see Association of Project Managers
Apple 35n5, 42
Aronovitch, H. 28–9
Arthur Andersen 68–9
assessment 84, 85, 137
Association of Project Managers (APM) 91n10

Beaver, Graham 128
behavior 18
benchmarking 81, 87, 88, 91n10
blended learning 85
blue ocean strategy 26–7
blueprints 21, 22, 142, 143

Boeing 35n4
Boone, Peter 9n9
borderless development 74
BP 78
brain-based learning 72
Brodie, Jim 67n7
budgets 100
Burke, Edmund 103
business development 21, 23, 24
business expertise 39, 41, 48, 49
business innovation 23; see also innovation
business models 13, 23, 24
business optimization 23
business system 11–13, 14, 16, 21, 23, 25, 35n1; Canon Academy 97–100; exploitation strategy 26; generic strategies 29, 30, 35; Mars University 60

Canon Academy 6, 92–102, 137–9; business system 97–100; company profile 93–5; future challenges 101; lessons learned 100–1; performance measurement 144–5; strategic profile 143–4; strategy formation 95–6; strategy specification 142–3
career development 84, 88, 137
case-based research 145–6
CEIB see China Europe International Business School
certification: Agfa Academy 117; Nokia 115; Philips Lighting University 7, 113, 119–22, 140
change: Canon Academy 97, 143; change management communication 88;

exceptional learning 35; Heineken University 46; Mars 4–5, 54; organizational flexibility 16; personal system 18–19; strategic 19; strategy implementation 28; *see also* transformation
Chevron 78
China 56, 114–15, 133
China Europe International Business School (CEIB) 114, 125
Cisco 115, 120, 126n2
classroom learning 49; Canon Academy 99–100; Deloitte University 71, 74–5; Shell Project Academy 83
Clegg, E. 133
coaching 84, 107, 137
co-creation 34, 101, 131
co-evolution 9n6
cognition 18
College strategy 25–6, 28–35, 134–41, 146
commitment 62, 63–4
communication 88
Communities of Practice (CoPs) 46
community building 15–16, 47, 48, 82, 84, 137
competencies 18, 39, 40; Canon Academy 93, 138; Deloitte University 73; Shell Project Academy 81, 82, 84, 90, 137
competition 26–7
competitive advantage 13, 34, 129, 131, 132–3
conferences 84
continuous learning 3, 19–24
cooperation 15
CoPs *see* Communities of Practice
corporate identity 39, 42, 49
corporate social responsibility 47, 130–1
corporate universities: definitions and concepts 7–8, 127, 128–32; future research 145–6; Learning Formats Model 4, 43–8, 49, 50; literature review 127, 132–3; number of 1, 9n1; as organizational units 129–30; philosophy 131–2; strategy 3, 8, 25–37, 130–1, 134–45, 147; top management support for 111; value creation 4, 38–43, 44–50; Van Hooydonk's journey 113–26
Corporate University Profiler 36n13, 51n20
costs: cost and revenue models 13; cost-to-income ratio 109, 112n9; Lean Six Sigma 105; Nokia 116; Shell Project Academy 86, 87, 89
course portfolios 85
CRH 40–1
cross-national comparative research 145–6

cultural issues 75
curricula: Agfa Academy 117; Canon Academy 96; Deloitte University 71, 73, 75; ING Business School 104, 110, 136; Mars University 60, 61; Philips Lighting University 140
customization 107, 112n8, 136
Customized Learning Group 33, 41, 64–5

De Alliantie 29–31, 36n9
De Geus, Arie 133, 148n15
Dealtry, Richard 133
decentralization 117, 124; Canon Academy 101; ING Bank Academy 108, 109; Mars University 54
Deloitte University 5, 68–76, 139–40; "As One Strategy" 69, 73–4; brain-based learning 73; business expertise 41; lessons learned 74–5; performance measurement 144–5; program governance structure 74; strategic profile 143–4; strategy specification 142–3
DHV University 31–2, 36n11, 40–1
differentiation 13
digital learning: decentralized content creation 124; Deloitte University 72, 74–5, 76; Philips Lighting University 119, 141; speed to knowledge 123; *see also* e-learning
Disney University 42
distance learning 85, 122–3
downstream activities 79
Ducati 129, 131–2, 148n11

economic crisis 1, 103, 107, 135
edu-gaming 115, 116, 121
Eichinger, Robert W. 67n8
Einstein, Albert 38
e-learning 46, 49, 123; Agfa Academy 116, 117; Canon Academy 99, 100; Deloitte University 71, 76; Mars University 60, 61; Nokia 114–15; Philips Lighting University 119, 121, 122, 140; *see also* digital learning
emotions 18, 72
employees: engagement 16, 62, 63–4, 145; ING Business School 104, 105, 145; Mars 55–6, 61, 62, 63–4; motivation of 120, 121; personal system 18–19; Philips Lighting University 120–2; Shell 79, 83, 84, 88; strategy development 23; strategy implementation 22; *see also* people
empowerment 117, 124, 142, 145; Mars University 60, 66; Philips Lighting University 119; pressures for 101

Index

Enclos Corp. 1
events 84, 87, 88, 89
Exademy 50n12
excellence 61–3
exceptional learning 19–21, 28, 29, 35, 135, 147; *see also* exploration
expatriates 79
experiential learning 4
expertise 39, 41, 48, 49
exploitation 3, 23, 26–8, 29, 31, 135; *see also* learning as usual
exploration 3, 21, 23, 26–8, 29, 31, 135; *see also* exceptional learning
Exploring learning format 43, 44
Exxon Mobil 78

Facebook 13, 131
feedback 44
financial crisis 103, 107, 135
Finland 115–16
"flash communities" 7, 123
flexibility 16
Franklin, Benjamin 1, 34, 36n17
FrieslandCampina 129, 130–1, 147n9

gaming 43, 44, 49, 123; Deloitte University 70, 76; Nokia 115, 116; Philips Lighting University 119, 121, 122, 140
Gazprom 78, 137
Gelb, Peter 10–11, 13–16
General Electric 1, 9n4
generic strategies 3, 9n5, 25, 28–35, 134–41
Gino, Francesca 132
Glaser, E.M. 8
global operations: Canon 93; Deloitte 69, 74, 75, 139; Mars 61
Gould, Karen 128
governance 85–6, 88, 137
guidelines 21, 22
Guttman, Howard 57

habits 18
Hamers, Ralph 109, 110
Haniel Academy 40–1, 50n9
health and wellbeing 72
Heineken 4, 45, 46, 48, 51n15; "Het Portaal" 131
high touch learning 49, 51n22
Hommen, Jan 107, 110
Huizinga, Nicoline 133
Hunter, Paul 53–67

"Ibansk effect" 91n12
IBS *see* ING Business School
ideal-types 28–9

identity 39, 42, 49
IHC Merwede 39–40
IKEA 129–30
imaging industry 92–3
individualized learning 124
industry knowledge 73
informal learning 34, 67n9, 119, 122, 123, 128, 131, 141
informal networks 15
ING Bank Academy 103–4, 107–11, 135–6
ING Business School (IBS) 6–7, 103–12, 135–6; performance measurement 144–5; strategic profile 143–4; strategy specification 142–3
innovation: Academy strategy 29, 30, 31, 35; business innovation 23; Deloitte University 41, 73
inside out strategy 50, 51n23
integration 146
International Project Management Association (IPMA) 84
Internet 84, 120, 122, 141; *see also* e-learning
inter-organizational learning 131–2
investment 77, 78, 80, 136
IPMA *see* International Project Management Association

Jobs, Steve 42

KAM *see* Key Account Management
Kennedy, John F. 147n1
Kenya Airlines 39–40
Key Account Management (KAM) 95, 98–9
Kim, Chan 26–7
knowledge: Canon Academy 97; Deloitte University 41, 73; generic strategies 30; knowledge creation 28; proof of 124; speed to 34, 114, 115, 118–19, 122, 123, 141; tacit 122, 123, 126n10
Knowles, Malcolm S. 25
Kolb, David 4, 44
Kuwait Petroleum Corporation 137, 148n16

Lafley, Alan 27
Le Guin, Ursula K. 113
leadership: Deloitte University 68, 70, 75; generic strategies 30; informal 15; ING Business School 104–5; market 69; Mars University 60, 61, 62, 63; Pixar 49; Shell Project Academy 82; strategy implementation 28; styles 26; TNT 47; *see also* top management
Leadership Pipeline concept 104–5

Lean Six Sigma 105
learning: Canon Academy 6, 96, 97, 99–102, 138; College strategy 30; continuous 3, 19–24; Deloitte University 5, 68, 70–3, 75–6, 139; by doing 99; Ducati 131–2; Heineken University 46; individualized 124; informal 34, 67n9, 119, 122, 123, 128, 131, 141; ING Bank Academy 108, 111; ING Business School 6–7, 105–6, 110; inter-organizational 131–2; literature review 132–3; Mars 4–5, 57, 58, 60, 64–6, 134–5; Nokia 114–15, 116; organizational flexibility 16; personal development 39; Philips Lighting University 7, 113, 118–23, 140–1; Pixar 49; School strategy 25, 29, 30, 34; Shell Project Academy 81–2, 85; technology impact on 7
learning as usual 19, 28, 29, 34, 137, 141; *see also* exploitation
learning cycle 44
Learning Formats Model 4, 43–8, 49, 50
learning management systems (LMSs): Agfa Academy 117; Canon Academy 99; Mars 60, 61, 62; performance measurement 145; Philips Lighting University 7, 120
learning organizations 133
LED technology 118, 119, 120, 121, 126n6–n8, 140, 148n17
LMSs *see* learning management systems
Lombardo, Michael M. 67n8

Managed Print Service (MPS) 99–100
management development 19, 31–2, 47, 60; *see also* leadership; talent development
market leadership 69
market system 11–13, 23
markets 26–7
Marks, J.B. 8
Mars, Forrest E., Sr. 54, 55, 63, 67n2
Mars University 4–5, 53–67, 57–66, 134–5; corporate identity 42; Customized Learning Group 33, 41, 64–5; Five Principles 42, 54, 55, 57, 58, 66; integration 146; lessons learned 65; origins and nature of the company 54–5; performance measurement 144–5; reinvention 58; strategic profile 143–4; strategic review 58–60; strategy specification 142–3; transformation plans and actions 60–4
Martin, Andre 58, 65, 67n7
Martin, Roger 27
mass customization 107, 112n8, 136
Mauborgne, René 26–7
Meister, Jeanne 128, 133

mentoring 84, 137
Metropolitan Opera, New York 10–11, 13–16
Meyer, Ron 10–24, 28, 35n1, 38–52
Michaels, Paul S. 53, 57, 66, 67n1
"The Milk Story" website 130–1
mission statements 143, 144, 148n20
mobile technologies 76, 115, 123
motivation 120, 121
MPS *see* Managed Print Service

NASA Project Academy 88
Netherlands 9n1, 103, 113, 129–30
networks: cross-unit 39, 40–1, 49; organizational system 15
New York Metropolitan Opera 10–11, 13–16
Nokia 7, 114–16, 124, 125
Nonaka, I. 126n10
norms 16

oil and gas industry 78–9
on-the-job training 83
organizational culture 16, 61, 66
organizational development 21, 39; Canon Academy 93, 96, 101; College strategy 30, 35
organizational learning 4, 147; Canon Academy 6, 93, 101, 138; cross-national comparative research 146; definition of 129; Deloitte University 139; FrieslandCampina 130; ING Bank Academy 108, 111; ING Business School 105, 107; learning as usual 34; literature review 132–3; Mars 4–5, 66; Philips Lighting University 7, 113, 118–19, 122, 140–1; Pixar 49; Shell Project Academy 137; Van Hooydonk 114
organizational structure 15, 26
organizational system 13–17, 21, 60, 146
outside-in strategy 50, 51n23
outsourcing 90

partnerships 131–2
Paton, R. 133
Pelster, Bill 5, 68–76
people: connecting 40–1, 42–3, 46, 48, 122–3; organizational system 15; people development 19; *see also* employees; stakeholders
performance 32–3; Mars 59; measurement 144–5; performance management systems 101; performance support 120, 122, 123; Shell Project Academy 86–8, 90

personal development: Shell Project Academy 82, 84, 88; value creation 39–40, 46–8, 49, 50
personal system 17, 18–19
Pertamina 39–40, 137
Petcare Academy, Mars 64–5
Petrobras 78
PetroChina 78
Petronas 137
Pfeffer, Jeffrey 35
Philips Lighting University 7, 33–4, 113–14, 117–23, 124, 125, 140–1; integration 146; performance measurement 144–5; strategic profile 143–4; strategy specification 142–3
Phillipps, Tim 73
Pisano, Gary 132
Pixar 48–9
plans, strategic 21, 22
PMI *see* Project Management Institute
Polanyi, M. 126n10
Polet, Ruud 103–12
Porter, Michael 9n5, 25
positions 18
Pride Center, Kenya Airlines 39–40
Prince, Christopher 128
professional development: Deloitte University 75, 139; Shell Project Academy 81, 84, 85, 90
program design 82–3
project delivery 81, 87, 90
project management 5–6, 71, 77, 80, 81–2, 84, 85
Project Management Institute (PMI) 90
Provoost, Rudy 118
"pull" approaches 7–8, 106, 113, 117, 119, 120–2, 123, 135
"push" approaches 7–8, 105–6, 120

Qiao, J.X. 133

Rademakers, Martyn 133
Raisch, S. 26
red ocean strategies 27
relational networks 15
Renaud-Coulon, Annick 133
resources 7, 11, 12, 30, 35
return on investment (ROI) 86, 90, 145
roadmaps 21, 22, 23
ROI *see* return on investment
Russian Railways (RZD) 1, 9n3
RWS 41, 50n11

Salzberg, Barry 70, 71, 75
School strategy 25–6, 28–35, 134–5, 136–7, 139–41, 146
self-organization 22
Senge, Peter M. 53, 132–3, 148n15
Sham, C. 133
Shell Project Academy (SPA) 5–6, 50n6, 77–91, 136–7; community-based approach 82; costs 86, 87, 89; critical success factors 88; Desired World in Project Land 81–2, 87; governance structure 85–6; integration 146; lessons learned 89–90; performance 86–8, 144–5; program design 82–3; project delivery process benchmark 81; SPA Pentagon 6, 83–5, 89, 137, 144; strategic profile 143–4; strategy specification 142–3; value creation 40, 42
Shepherd, Jon 5, 58
simulations 47, 49, 70, 76
Skype 13
social media 101
SPA *see* Shell Project Academy
stakeholders: Deloitte University 74, 75, 139; FrieslandCampina 130–1; Mars 54, 55; organizational system 15; *see also* people
Starbucks 120, 126n9
strategic frameworks 21, 22
strategy 8, 25–37, 134–45, 147; Canon 6, 93, 95–6, 97, 98, 100, 101–2, 137–9, 142–4; continuous alignment of 11–19, 23, 24; as continuous learning 3, 21–2, 23–4; corporate university as key component of 130–1; definition of 129; Deloitte 69–70, 73–4, 139–40, 142–4; development 21, 23, 24, 25; focus 25–6, 32; generic 3, 9n5, 25, 28–35, 134–41; implementation 19–22, 25, 28, 31, 98, 102, 138; ING Business School 103, 104–6, 110, 135–6, 142–4; literature review 132–3; Mars 4, 55, 57, 58, 65, 134–5, 142–4; Philips Lighting University 140–1, 142–4; renewal 6, 7, 25, 30, 31–2, 35; Shell Project Academy 77, 136–7, 142–4; specificity 21–2, 142–3; strategic profile 143–4
sustainability services 73–4
Sutton, Robert 35
synergies 40, 58, 146; ING Bank Academy 108; Mars 135; Shell Project Academy 90

Takeuchi, H. 126n10
talent development: Ahold 46–7; Deloitte University 71, 74, 75; ING Bank Academy 109; ING Business School 106;

Pixar 49; Shell Project Academy 82, 88; TNT 47
team spirit 15–16, 48
technology 7, 123; Canon 96, 138; Deloitte University 70, 75–6; LED 118, 119, 120, 121, 126n6–n8, 140, 148n17; *see also* digital learning; e-learning
Termeer, Carin 103–12
Tilmant, Michel 104, 110, 112n4
TNT 4, 45, 47–8, 51n17
top management: Canon 95, 96–7, 100, 102, 138, 143; direct and regular contact with 143, 144; Heineken University 46; ING Bank Academy 109; ING Business School 108; Mars 57, 63; Philips Lighting University 140; relationship with corporate university 111; Shell Project Academy 85–6, 89, 90; TNT 47–8; *see also* leadership
Torchio, Gabriele del 132
Total 78
training: Agfa Academy 117; Ahold Retail Academy 47; Deloitte University 70; Disney University 42; Heineken University 46; learning formats 43, 44; Mars 56, 57–8, 60, 64–5; Nokia 114; on-the-job 83; Philips Lighting University 120, 122; Shell Project Academy 82, 83
transformation 3, 27, 28, 29, 60–4, 66, 135; *see also* change
transformational learning 21, 28, 29, 35, 138, 140–1, 147
Treacy, Michael 25, 32
Twitter 131

United States (US) 9n1, 133
upstream activities 79
user-generated content 101, 117, 131

value capture 13
value chain 11, 12, 23, 30
value creation 45–8, 49–50, 111; business innovation 23; business system 11; ING Business School 107; Value Creation Menu 4, 38–43, 44–5
value proposition 11, 12, 13, 23, 24; "Disney experience" 42; generic strategies 30, 32, 34, 35; Mars University 60
values: Deloitte 71; Mars 54, 55, 57
Van Dam, Nick 68–76
Van der Molen, Ronald 95, 96–7, 98–9, 100
Van der Pool, Han 38–52
Van der Veer, Jeroen 81
Van Hooydonk, Stefaan 7, 113–26, 140–1
Van Ooijen, Frank 131
video clips 115–16
virtual learning 71, 76, 116
vision 21, 22, 132, 142, 143
Vlerick Management School 114, 116
VolkerWessels Academy 40–1, 42–3

Walton, John 128
Weber, Max 36n6
webinars 70, 76, 115, 116, 119, 122, 140
Wheeler, Kevin 128, 133
Wierda, Hans 77–91
Wiersema, Fred 25, 32
wikis 119, 121, 124, 140
work streams 60

Yahoo! 36n15

Zinovjev, Alexander 91n12